DERELICTION of DUTY

The Failed Presidency of Donald John Trump

Frederic B. Hill

For "Mac" Mathias

- who placed country and conscience before party or person

Cover Photo: Contrast in Character. Donald Trump being interviewed by Fox News in front of the Lincoln Memorial, May 3, 2020

Credit: Photo by Oliver Contreras/Pool/Abaca Press

Copyright © 2020 Frederic B. Hill

More Comments on *Dereliction of Duty*

"With skill and dispatch, rapier and broadsword, Hill brings his finely honed reportorial and editorial skills to bear on our national civic disaster, pungently echoing the clarion call of Maine's Senator Margaret Chase Smith from decades ago, "Wake up America!" Her words reverberate with power and majesty throughout this eagerly awaited book by an award winning journalist. Hill provides all voters in 2020 with a most disturbing portrait of a president out of control and careening wildly about - unchecked."

Christian Potholm, author of The Delights of Democracy.

"This book is truly the 'first draft of history' of a major testing time for our institutions. This collection of essays on the events of the past few years and the implications of Donald Trump's policies and governing style provides voters with a firmer grip on the stakes in the 2020 elections."

James E. Goodby, Ambassador (Ret.), Distinguished Service Professor Emeritus, Carnegie Mellon University.

"Fred Hill is an astute student of history, culture and politics, with a deep understanding of national security and international affairs. He skewers his targets with lively, passionate and pointed prose – often aimed directly at President Trump – and frequently infuses a sense of humor into his commentary that makes the hard truths easier to read."

Tricia Bishop, director of opinion content, The Baltimore Sun.

"Insightful commentary on the evolving national turmoil generated by our unfit President."

Tom Allen, former Maine Congressman.

"Fred Hill's experience gives him a unique perspective on world affairs. He is an especially astute observer of the current administration."

Susan Young, Editorial page editor, Bangor Daily News.

"Congress shall make no law…..abridging the freedom of speech or of the press….." First Amendment, Bill of Rights; December 15, 1791.

"The enemy of the people"- a phrase used by authoritarian and totalitarian rulers throughout history, most notably by Josef Stalin, dictator of the Soviet Union, to justify the murder of thousands, from party leaders to peasants.

"The fake news media, (including The New York Times, Washington Post, major news networks – except Fox) *"are the enemy of the American people."* President Donald John Trump, American Conservative Action Conference, February 24, 2017 (and hundreds of times since).

"The price of greatness is responsibility. The people of the United States cannot escape responsibility." Winston Churchill, at Harvard, 1943.

"I don't take responsibility at all." Donald John Trump, March 13, 2020 - when asked about the federal government's poor response to the need for testing kits as the Covid-19 pandemic escalated in the United States.

"The larger the mob, the harder the test. As democracy is perfected, we move toward a lofty ideal. On some great and glorious day, the plain folks of the land will reach their heart's desire at last, and the White House will be adorned by a downright moron."

Henry Louis Mencken, *Baltimore Evening Sun*, 1920

- comment on the Harding-Cox presidential election

CONTENTS

All done before it starts: The GOP way to deal with impeachment of a president.

Credit: © 2019 Walt Handelsman – Distributed by Tribune Content Agency, LLC

Foreword

Senator Chris Van Hollen

America's standing in the world is undeniably tied to its position as a beacon of democracy on the world stage. The hallmarks of our country are what many aspire to -- grounded in our pursuit of freedom, democratic values, moral leadership, and a more perfect union. We recognize that we have a long journey ahead before we can fully achieve the goal of equal rights and equal justice, but those ideals remain our guiding lights and they are an inspiration to others around the world. Not only have we worked to implement these principles here at home, they have also formed the basis for much of our foreign policy. At least since the end of World War II, we have held the conviction that a world that embraces those same principles — and builds the institutions to promote and protect them — not only serves our interests, but helps to achieve a more peaceful and prosperous world.

Fred Hill knows this well and deeply values our American democracy and ideals along with their impact worldwide. His career has been defined by an ability to provide clear-eyed examinations of the conduct of leaders in this country to hold them accountable. He is driven by a true sense of how vital, honest and robust reporting is to the health and welfare of our country.

In his lifetime, Fred has had several careers that place him in a rare position to bear witness to the conduct of government at the highest level. As a journalist for *The Baltimore Sun*, he uncovered extensive corruption in Maryland and played a role in the resignation of Vice-President Spiro Agnew, covered civil wars in Africa, a revolution in Iran and the conclaves of popes, and penned editorials on foreign affairs. I met Fred when he was a senior adviser to a leading Republican senator, Charles McC. Mathias, Jr., where he skillfully navigated policy and politics on Capitol Hill and helped pass historic legislation such as the anti-Apartheid Act on South Africa with overwhelming bipartisan support over the veto of a popular president.

And later he led an office in the Department of State that staged wargaming exercises on national security challenges for senior officials - looking ahead to future challenges like the possible collapse of the Soviet Union, nuclear ambitions of Iran and North Korea, and critical global issues such as water and energy resources. At the State Department, Fred held himself to the highest standard working without any political bias to explore the most complex threats to the national interests of the United States – under the Republican administrations of Ronald Reagan, George H. W. Bush, and George W. Bush, and the Democratic administration of William Jefferson Clinton.

These wide-ranging experiences provide Fred with a singular lens to view the world, but also an in-depth appreciation for the profound impact America's standing has on our foreign policy and national security. With that perspective, Fred distinctively assesses and writes about the presidency of Donald Trump – with clarity and concern for the basic values of our nation, its Constitution and the vital role of the rule of law, the separation of powers, and a free press.

Fred's experience living and working in these institutions is complemented by the deep reverence he holds for their place in American life. It comes as no surprise that he has found the 45th president of the United States repeatedly falling short and even exhibiting a dereliction of duty as our commander in chief. Having covered corruption in Maryland and the Watergate scandal of the Nixon years, having traveled the world as a foreign correspondent and navigated the dynamics on Capitol Hill and then the powerful forces in the executive branch in examining critical national security issues at the State Department, he has a deep understanding of American governance, the levers of power in our democracy, and the corrupting capacity of some to abuse that power.

Not surprisingly, he has been appalled, like so many Americans, by Trump's willingness to deepen the political polarization in the country, exploit racial tensions, demean hard-working professionals in government service such as the diplomatic corps, the intelligence community, and the federal workforce. And as someone who has been deeply engaged in foreign affairs, he was stunned by Trump's embrace of Russia and readiness to undermine alliances that had won the Cold War and supported international institutions since World War II, not to mention his erratic policies towards Iran and North Korea.

And as a journalist for so many years before joining the government, Fred was repulsed by a president who lacks an appreciation for the role of an independent and free press – repeatedly using a favorite phrase of Soviet dictator Joseph Stalin to call "the enemy of the people" any member or newspaper or media outlet that criticized him. This flies in the face of a key pillar of our democracy that has been valued since the birth of this nation.

Lucky for us, retirement has allowed Fred to return to writing - the basic thread of his life's work. With his thoughtful insights, this book makes for a captivating read with a collection of op-ed articles and commentary from Dallas to Baltimore, Seattle to Maine, that not only reflect the extensive breadth of his knowledge of government and matters of national security, but also offers a vigorous and timely account of the last four years in the United States.

Dereliction of Duty paints an accurate picture of the clear and present danger Trump's presidency is to our country at home and abroad. Even amidst the pervasive polarization in politics today, this is something all Americans, regardless of party, should read with deep concern. Fred reminds us of all that is at stake in November if this reckless administration gets the chance to continue on its path of destruction against our democratic ideals and the rule of law. - July 14, 2020

Preface

A Political Evolution

Despite disbelief from some Republican friends, I actually have been a registered Republican three times – once in profound innocence and twice for tactical reasons. But I have been a middle-of-the-road Democrat most of my life, yet largely passive during separate careers in journalism and government.

As a government major at Bowdoin College, I was immersed in American history, constitutional law and political theory, from Aristotle to Machiavelli to Jefferson, and not contemporary local or national politics. (I will be forever thankful to several professors and a curriculum that instilled a deep respect for the rule of law, our basic freedoms and values of speech and religion, and human rights).

In the summer of 1960, after my second year at Bowdoin, I went west to play summer baseball in Oregon. But a stop with a friend near Stanford University led to a detour to visit another friend in Los Angeles. He and I then went to the 1960 Democratic convention and got lucrative jobs cleaning the convention hall at night after the close of each day's hysteria. In addition, I learned how I could gain possession of an automobile, by agreeing to chauffeur various political figures during the day. I'm not sure when I slept – but I was 20 years old.

And who did I end up driving around for three or four days? Ross Barnett, the nasty segregationist governor of Mississippi. Barnett and his henchmen loved that he was being chauffeured by a young Yankee - despite the fact that I was able to argue with him about the South's racist history, the Civil War and quote from a couple of William Faulkner's withering profiles of Barnett's own back country – such as the evil and rapacious Snopes clan portrayed in the marvelous trilogy, *The Hamlet, The Town and The Mansion.*

I voted, I think, for Richard Nixon that fall – an act I've generally forgotten. Even when I took my first real job as a young reporter at The Baltimore Sun in 1965 after a brief detour in law school, I was still, nominally, a Republican. I actually enjoyed a certain celebrity status in the center-city district where I first lived. Maryland was and still is a very Democratic state, but most of the Republicans in that urban neighborhood were African-Americans. And in an ironic twist on my brief stint with Governor Barnett, let's say, I stood out.

As a reporter, foreign correspondent and editorial writer at The Sun for 20 years, I took no active role in politics, though I generally voted Democratic.

In the spring of 1985, that changed - somewhat. Senator Charles "Mac" Mathias, an engaging, intellectual and popular moderate Republican, asked me to join his staff as his director of foreign affairs. An inviting opportunity; I agreed. It was one of the most exciting and memorable periods of my life, even though the senator decided not to run again in 1986.

In the 18 months I worked for him, we accomplished a great deal. With a deputy who is today far more known, Chris Van Hollen, now one of Maryland's two senators, we worked under Mac's leadership to play a major role in passage of the extraordinary anti-Apartheid Act, passed over President Reagan's veto with 31 GOP members defying presidential pressure (including a young senator named McConnell); we gained approval of arms control measures; we wrote many op-ed articles for leading publications. I accompanied Mathias on an extraordinary five-week trip to the Middle East, where we had interviews with almost all the leaders of the most important countries: King Hussein (Jordan), Hosni Mubarak (Egypt), co-premiers Rabin and Shamir (Israel), and the foreign ministers of Saudi Arabia and Syria. In the midst of the grim Iran-Iraq war across the Persian/Arab Gulf, we flew over the vulnerable Saudi oil fields.

After the senator's retirement, I joined the Department of State to establish its first office to conduct gaming exercises (simulations) on potential national security threats and global issues. An interesting and challenging job – and one in which I remained for another 20 years. I worked in three Republican administrations and one Democratic administration with concern only for examining the toughest challenges to the national security of the country - not the interests of any party.

We focused on nuclear weapons, transitions in governments such as the potential collapse of the Soviet Union, political-military clashes (India-Pakistan, the Koreas, Bosnia), terrorism and emerging global issues such as water resources and energy. A decade or two before they emerged as critical issues, we examined Iran's nuclear ambitions, tensions in the South China sea and the potential for clashes over water resources in the Middle East.

I was appalled when a Republican-led House headed by Newt Gingrich shut down the government in its confrontation with the Clinton administration. But I remained apolitical.

That certainly changed when I retired in 2006. I did not have to retire, but I had become frustrated with the State Department bureaucracy and the Bush/Cheney foreign policy, especially its decision to go to war in Iraq.

At the request of senior State department officials, my office had conducted a day-long "wargame" and discussion on Iraq in October, 2002, five months before the invasion. Our conclusions, from 35 of the leading experts on Iraq and the region, not only argued that such an invasion would be a disaster but also sent six telling recommendations to Secretary of State Colin Powell that were ignored by the administration. The most fateful was a virtually unanimous view by all participants that the Iraqi army should not be disbanded after the certain overthrow of Saddam Hussein.

The Bush/Cheney disbanding of the main cohorts of the Iraqi army shortly after Saddam's fall led directly to the deadly onslaught on American forces by Al Qaeda in Iraq and other forces, its instability and, eventually, the creation of ISIS. I filed an official dissent with Secretary Powell through the department's private dissent channel, established during the Vietnam war.

I was ready to leave, and did a few years later. Upon moving to Maine, I found a ready audience for critical commentary. I wrote a column on foreign affairs for the *Bangor Daily News* for several years, and then for other newspapers, including *The Baltimore Sun* and *The Dallas Morning News*.

Through syndication, the articles have appeared in newspapers across the country, from Seattle to New York.

I was not particularly partisan. One column before the 2008 presidential election concluded that George H. W. Bush, a Republican, had been the most effective president in foreign policy since Eisenhower.

It was not a difficult choice. With smart, balanced and strategic advisers such as Brent Scowcroft and James Baker, Bush 41 handled the collapse of the Soviet empire with restraint, put together a strategic coalition to defeat Saddam Hussein's invasion of Kuwait and dealt with Israel's settlements policy with hard-headed pragmatism.

In 2008, I also devoted a column to assessing the strengths of then Sen. Barack Obama and Sen. John McCain on a wide range of issues. I gave Obama a narrow edge – before

McCain's disastrous gamble in choosing Sarah Palin as his running-mate. I criticized Obama from time to time, especially over his indecision on Syria.

Meanwhile, I did take a plunge into active politics for the first time.

Several friends and I, all Democrats, switched registration in Maine's 2010 election for governor to support the person most qualified to be the governor, but he lost in the primary. I did the same briefly in 2019 to oppose Sen. Susan Collins, a Trump apologist.

I took part in two campaigns for Democratic candidates. I worked on the 2016 campaign in Maryland to support my former colleague, then Rep. Van Hollen, who won the Senate seat once held by Senator Mathias for three terms. And in 2018, I worked for a young former Marine, Jared Golden, who defeated the last GOP member of the House in New England to win Maine's conservative second district.

Since then, I have focused on my family, several books and playing golf and squash. I did not seek to write a lot of op-ed articles. Yet the dizzying destruction of the American political and social fabric by Donald John Trump day after day continued to demand some response, even though many more brilliant minds were tracking his ineptitude, insults, corruption, racism and ruination of our place in the world – right through a continuing reckless foreign policy, the tragicomic impeachment trial and Trump's denial, delay and costly indecision in dealing with the Covid-19 crisis.

And in the midst of that last catastrophe, Trump sought to exploit the racial tensions that erupted after the murder of George Floyd, a black man, by a white police officer in Minneapolis. The most respected military leaders in the country, including former generals James Mattis and Colin Powell, and the serving and past chairmen of the Joint Chiefs, condemned Trump's abuse of the military to subdue peaceful protestors.

Many respected critics have condemned Trump and what he has done to America. George Packer compared Trump's response to the pandemic as equal to that of a Belarus or a Pakistan - an administration "too corrupt or stupid to head off mass suffering." Contrasting Trump to earlier American leaders, David Brooks, an independent Republican, noted "right now, we don't have a leader. We have ……a damaged narcissist unable to see the true existence of other human beings except insofar as they are good or bad for himself."

Commentators in pro-American countries were appalled. An Irish Times columnist wrote: "The country Trump promised to make great again has never in its history seemed so pitiful."

For my part, I have now found it virtually impossible to capture the totality of Trump's incompetence. Essentially, he is a little man, a serial liar, a corrupt, flim-flam artist, insecure bully and Russian-assisted accidental president with not one redeeming quality, a man who cares only about himself – the nation, its 328 million citizens and the world be damned. - July 4, 2020

Part I: "I Know More than the Generals"

Like many Americans, I did not take Donald J. Trump seriously in 2016. He was a carnival barker, a TV-reality showman who bragged about abusing women and routinely lied about his past, called climate change "a Chinese hoax."

I only began to pay much attention when 50 national security experts, *all Republicans,* signed a letter reported in The New York Times that argued that Trump, if elected, would prove to be "the most dangerous" and "most reckless" president in American history. That was August 9, 2016.

The signatories included several leaders I knew and admired: Michael Hayden, former director of the Central Intelligence Agency, Robert Zoellick, former World Bank president, Eliot Cohen, a smart strategist and two Homeland Security directors for George W. Bush. *All Republicans!*

That letter, making observations now painfully accurate, said: (Trump) "is unable and unwilling to separate truth from falsehood. He lacks self-control, and acts impetuously. He cannot take personal criticism. All of these are dangerous qualities."

A Trump list of his top five advisers on national security was revealing. All five were truly obscure; one was a little-known general; another was practically living in Moscow.

But even generals were no match for Trump, a five-time draft dodger, who bragged "I know more about ISIS than the generals."

I watched the debates between Trump and Hillary Clinton. I was no fan of Clinton, and recognized her mistakes such as maintaining a private email server while she was Secretary of State - something even Colin Powell had done. But given a reasonably positive record as Secretary, I assumed most Americans would recognize that she had far more experience and intelligence than her opponent.

Yet, astonished by Trump's electoral college victory as many, I can't say I was unduly alarmed by his ascension to the highest office in the land. I assumed, blindly perhaps, he would become more balanced, rise to the occasion.

****

Until a few days after the election, and most certainly on Inauguration day, January 20, 2017, when he gave the most disgraceful presidential address in modern history.

Not only did he fail to even try to lift a nation's spirits, he did not offer the slightest sign that he understood the enormous responsibilities he was assuming. With the dreadful monotone that has come to be the headlight of his mental limitation – he talked of how he alone could fix "American carnage." Bypassing any reference to American values and traditions, Trump talked mostly about himself and lashed out at the very establishment that made him somewhat rich – though much of his relative wealth was due to deceit, corruption and Russian money.

And within 24 hours, he proceeded to show his true
character – insecure, narcissistic and as dangerous as the 50
Republican national security experts had warned.

Watching television, as he seems to spend half his life doing,
now President Trump ordered advisers to prove that the
networks and newspapers were wrong in saying that the
crowds at his inauguration were much smaller than
President Obama's – despite clear evidence they were.

He continued to rant and rave that he had won the popular
vote – despite the fact that all conclusive results showed that
Clinton had received three million more votes.

He demanded establishment of a commission to investigate
the election results in all states; he claimed that illegal
immigrants accounted for his popular loss. The commission
never gained traction, with many states ignoring its
demands, and eventually fell by the wayside like so many
Trump threats.

It wasn't much longer before I concluded that a petulant
child had been elected president of the United States. I
recalled a comment about Trump by my favorite American
historian during the campaign, David McCullough, author
of biographies of Harry Truman and John Adams. Trump,
McCullough said: "A monstrous clown, with a monstrous
ego."

I hoped it wouldn't be true. And despite misgivings, I
actually gave Trump the benefit of the doubt when I
co-wrote a first column about his presidency, when he

selected the chief executive of Exxon, Rex Tillerson, as
Secretary of State. I offered "a clean slate." It didn't take long
to be shattered.

The first year offered plenty of evidence of disaster and
incompetence – from turmoil in the White House, to
revelations of more sexual affairs and secret payoffs to a
pathological obsession to reverse major accomplishments of
Barack Obama.

The new president's vows to block immigration were
studded with insults and threats against Mexicans and
Muslims. His vitriol encouraged white supremacist groups,
leading to deadly violence in Charlottesville, Virginia - after
which he placed blame "on all sides." Even his closest aides
did not agree with him. His base racism was clear. He
withdrew from the Paris Climate accord, and later the Iran
nuclear deal, and repeatedly insulted our nation's closest
allies. He tried – but failed - to replace Obama's health care
law.

The first year ended with a 35-day partial shutdown of the
government, triggered in large part by Trump's demands to
build a wall on the southern border with Mexico, a wall
most experts said was not needed.

It was not long before another fed-up insider in the White
House quit, and reported that Trump spent much of his day
watching Fox News and tweeting. This was a president?

The most revealing – and disturbing - incident in Trump's
first year came during a top-level Pentagon briefing for

Trump on crucial national security matters. Trump, who gained five draft exemptions due to alleged "bonespurs," had a child-like tantrum and called the nation's top generals and admirals "dopes" and "babies," and said he would never go to war with them. It was right after that briefing that Secretary of State Tillerson, the son of a combat veteran, said "He's a fucking moron." (1).

Barely a day has gone by in three and a half years when Donald John Trump has not proved the accuracy of Tillerson's assessment of his temperament and character. And now the nation has suffered deeply – perhaps irretrievably - from the contemptible, erratic behavior of a supreme narcissist who has been ranked as the worst president in American history by the American Political Science Association.

<u>ARTICLES</u>

<u>Trump's Focus on ISIS Reveals His Ignorance</u> **<u>– *The Baltimore Sun; September 9, 2016*</u>**

Donald Trump's accusation that President Barack Obama and Hillary Clinton are "founders of ISIS" is not only a good example of his reckless fear-mongering but also his complete lack of understanding about true threats to national security.

ISIS, or the Islamic State, as this brutal jihadist group is known, is not even the first, second, third or fourth most serious threat to the United States despite what Mr. Trump shouts from the stump with abandon.

First of all, ISIS grew out of the group al-Qaida in Iraq, which did not even exist until the Bush/Cheney invasion of Iraq in 2003. As to the withdrawal of U.S. forces from Iraq, completed under President Obama, the agreement to take that step was negotiated by President George W. Bush.

Secondly, Mr. Trump's references to San Bernardino and Orlando are woefully misplaced. Both incidents, while tragic, had as much to do with mental health conditions and outlandish access to automatic weapons as they did with terrorism. Furthermore, the worst terrorist incident in the United States other than 9/11 — the 1995 bombing of the Oklahoma City federal building, which killed 168 people — was committed by a Christian fundamentalist, the very kind of extremist Mr. Trump encourages with his hateful rhetoric.

As for threats to national security, Mr. Trump's truly clueless grasp of international affairs is reflected in irresponsible linkage of terrorism and crime to Muslims and immigrants. No country is immune from mindless acts of madness committed by people who have no respect for human life and civilized values. But U.S. counter-terrorism and law enforcement authorities since 9/11, under both the Bush and Obama administrations, have done a very good job of surveillance, investigation and prevention in a country of 320 million people.

In a huge, diverse country such as this, anything is quite possible, as the 9/11 attack demonstrated 15 years ago Sunday. But the gravest threats to American security, and the security of the industrialized West, come from several more complex challenges coming out of Russia, North Korea, Pakistan, the Middle East and China.

Mitt Romney declared Russia as the most serious threat facing the U.S. four years ago. While his campaign faltered badly, he seems to have had a crystal ball in that regard. Under Vladimir Putin, Russia, a country with a vast arsenal of nuclear weapons, has become more aggressive in the last few years: annexing Crimea, sending its troops into Ukraine, flying reckless flights over the Baltics and, as far as can be determined, trying to intervene in our current election with cyber attacks.

Russia's behavior is convenient for Mr. Trump to ignore since Paul Manafort, one of his revolving door of campaign managers, proved to have accepted millions of dollars to be a hand-maiden of Russian policy to undermine the stability of Ukraine. Mr. Trump's smirky compliments of Mr. Putin, his business dealings with Russians and his dismissal of the importance of NATO are grounds for suspicion of his friendly attitude toward Moscow. His latest embrace of Putin during Wednesday's veterans forum — praising an authoritarian leader with near-dictatorial powers as a stronger "leader" than his own president — verges on treason, a word that means disloyalty in betraying one's country.

North Korea, the most isolated country on earth, also poses a far more serious concern for U.S. and international stability than ISIS. Hundreds of thousands of armed troops, including more than 25,000 American forces, are lined up on both sides of a long border as a young and unproven new leader of the hermit kingdom uses the threat of a missile attack to retain his power.

Pakistan's internal instability ranks close to North Korea as another constant concern. The threat of both war with India, a war that could easily see the use of nuclear weapons, and Pakistan's willingness to create turmoil in neighboring Afghanistan, are grave matters.

The general instability and failure of governance in the Middle East also poses a far more serious threat to the international community than ISIS, now losing ground but still capable of conducting murderous acts. Syria's tragic civil war, Iraq's turmoil, unrest in Libya, Iran's hostility to the West (not just the U.S.) and potential instability in Saudi Arabia add up to a major strategic challenge.

And China's emergence as an up-and-coming world power could pose a long-term threat, especially given its current stance regarding the South China Sea.

Mr. Trump's lack of understanding of national security and international affairs in general prompted Brent Scowcroft, national security adviser to President George H. W. Bush, a widely admired strategic thinker, and Richard Armitage, deputy secretary of state to Colin Powell, both to denounce him. They had to be revolted by Trump's ridiculous boast: "I know more about ISIS than the generals."

And more than 50 officials who held senior positions in Republican administrations have condemned him as completely unsuited to be commander in chief. Mr. Trump "has little understanding of the nation's vital national interests," they said, and would be "the most reckless president in American history."

We must respect and heed their warning.

"Climate Change is a Chinese Hoax."

Credit: George Danby, Bangor Daily News

<u>Trump's Denial of Climate Change Alone Disqualifies Him for the Presidency – *Bangor Daily News* with Walter Kozumbo; October 17, 2016</u>

If possible, put aside Donald Trump's hate for minorities, his refusal to release his tax returns on billions in income, his draft deferments and his repugnant insults of women.

Put aside his ignorance of foreign affairs — the man who said " I know more than the generals" was described as " a national disgrace" by a real general, Colin Powell — and his traitorous embrace of Russia's Vladimir Putin.

There is one single issue that proves that Trump is unqualified to be president: his repeated claim that global warming and climate change are a hoax. He has repeated that line many times, and again in one of his many lies, he says he never said it.

On Nov. 6, 2012, Trump said on Twitter that " The concept of global warming was created by the Chinese to make U.S. manufacturing non-competitive." In January 2014, he tweeted to NBC News: " Is the country still spending money on the GLOBAL WARMING HOAX?" Then last year, he repeated " I don't believe in climate change."

Now, Trump's position should not be too surprising. Although he differs with the GOP on some issues, many Republicans think global warming — the well-documented historic increases in temperatures, sea level rise and oceanic acidification as well as reductions in Arctic Sea ice and snow cover — is a hoax.

Ignoring the 97 percent consensus among world climate scientists, the National Academy of Sciences and the United Nations Intergovernmental Panel on Climate Change, Trump and the GOP would rather echo the chants of organizations skeptical of global warming and funded by the fossil fuel industries than do what is right. Such blatant disregard for the truth in the face of overwhelming evidence suggests complete ignorance or total indifference to the potentially catastrophic threat of climate change.

As rising seas endanger coastal nations, imagine the chaotic effects of displacing millions of people worldwide. Hungry, desperate migrants seeking shelter, food and livelihood are likely to resort to violent and unlawful means to save themselves and their families. If not violence, then death from starvation and disease from infections would claim lives. The European migration crisis, a result of Syria's civil war, would pale in significance to the dire consequences of climate change.

President Barack Obama and Hillary Clinton are right to consider climate change the leading long-term threat. A safe and prosperous future demands adherence to facts, prioritization of threats and development of a comprehensive action plan. Human existence will depend upon it as global warming induces mass migrations that could trigger conflict, even use of nuclear weapons.

Another climate-related issue that demonstrates how the tea-party-tied GOP hurts the national interest is its opposition to ratification of the Law of the Sea Treaty. Almost all nations have approved the treaty, and the United States has less leverage in negotiations to determine the boundaries of the Arctic Ocean because the GOP prevents ratification.

The willingness of Trump and the GOP to deny overwhelming scientific evidence and the reality of climate change not only hinders international efforts but also blocks the ability of the U.S. government — the world's leader — to take preventive steps to plan for major improvements in infrastructure for coastal cities and regions.

At a meeting of the eight-nation Arctic Council in Portland this month, Maine Sen. Angus King highlighted the need to recognize the threat of climate change to enable planning for massive infrastructure needs. After hearing a Maine scientist predict that the melting of global ice sheets could drive up sea levels a foot in the next 15 years, King said, "Pretty scary. Imagine an extra foot of water in Scarborough Marsh."

Sadly, climate change is not the only major issue that has suffered from dishonest treatment by candidates and the media. The rampant lack of truthfulness in this presidential election is dismaying but increasingly common in the age of instant and superficial coverage. As George Orwell said, "Political language is designed to make lies sound truthful and murder respectable, and to give the appearance of solidity to pure wind."

A good question we may hear from our grandchildren in a couple of decades, as the Arctic Ocean is full of tourist ships and oil tankers, Atlantic Coast cities and beaches are underwater, insect-carrying diseases spread northward and polar bears are an afterthought, "Grandpa, did you vote for that guy who called climate change a Chinese hoax?"

<u>**Lying is Often Part of Politics, but Trump Has Taken It to New Heights**</u>
<u>**– *The Baltimore Sun*; November 2, 2016**</u>

Italian Renaissance philosopher Nicolo Machiavelli advised all political leaders to be willing to lie, to deceive, when necessary — to be a combination of lion and fox, using "cunning and strength, fraud and force." It appears modern politicians have taken the suggestion to new levels.

While opinions vary on which of the 43 men who have been president told the most or biggest lies, LBJ and Richard Nixon — from the Vietnam war to Watergate — usually rank pretty high. In more recent history, Bill Clinton, (no "sexual relations with that woman") and Ronald Reagan (Iran-Contra) also rate right up there. But nothing matches the current presidential campaign for its lies.

And ironically, it is the candidate who has called others liars with abandon who amounts to the biggest liar of all: Donald Trump.

The Democratic candidate, Hillary Clinton, certainly has told some whoppers, including tall tales regarding her use of a private email server while she was secretary of state. But it is Mr. Trump who wins the George Orwell award for his use — or abuse — of dishonesty. It was Orwell who said "Political language is designed to make lies sound truthful and murder respectable."

In fact, Mr. Trump has been so full of baloney, he is in a class by himself, comparing closely with the fascist slurs and outright falsehoods of Sen. Joseph McCarthy in the red-baiting days of the mid-20th century. A kernel of objective truth is usually at the base of many political lies, but not in the case of McCarthy or most of Mr. Trump's utterances. It is not surprising that they shared a political adviser, New York lawyer Roy Cohn.

On a practical level, political fact-checkers have found Mr. Trump committed far more falsehoods during the campaign and debates than Ms. Clinton. But check the truly outrageous lies of the GOP candidate.

Start with the "birther" lie, which even Mr. Trump now admits was false — five years after he seized on the right-wing charge that President Barack Obama was not born in the United States. In denouncing the claim in September, he dared to put forth another lie, blaming Ms. Clinton for the start of the rumor.

Then there are his claims to be a brilliant businessman, which ignore the silver spoon he was born with, along with his multiple bankruptcies and lifetime of fleecing of one contractor after another. Coupled with his recent refusal to release his tax returns, and you see his real business skill is hiding facts.

Mr. Trump's statement that "nobody has more respect for women" than he does has been repeatedly torn down by women coming forward with stories of being assaulted by him, not to mention that now infamous recording of his claim that celebrity gives him carte blanche to grope women.

His economic plan would cost $10 trillion, reduce taxes for only the wealthy and wipe out 3 million jobs, not help poor people, as he says. He clearly doesn't "know more about ISIS than the generals"; was actually in favor of the Iraq War early on, not against it as he says; and has in fact claimed on several occasions that global warming is a "hoax" created by the Chinese, despite his protestations that he has not.

The list seems endless. Donald Trump is, simply, a serial liar. For all her faults, the same cannot be said of Ms. Clinton.

Adolf Hitler and his propaganda wizard built much of their rationalization for World War II and persecution of the Jews on a technique known as "the big lie" — telling falsehoods so big and doing it so frequently that they are accepted simply because it's unbelievable that anyone could lie so brazenly.

Henry A. Murray, author of a 1943 psychological study of Adolf Hitler for the U.S. Office of Strategic Services — one that predicted his suicide — summed up the Nazi leader's use of lies: "Never admit a fault or a wrong; never accept blame, concentrate on one enemy at a time, blame that enemy for everything that goes wrong, and take advantage of every opportunity to raise a political whirlwind."

Sound familiar?

Mr. Trump is not Hitler, though many have portrayed him as having similar tendencies, and he has repeatedly embraced the telling of a "big lie."

There is a more appropriate word for his behavior, however, according to the Webster's and Oxford dictionaries:

Trumpery — def. Fraud, deception. A noun originally from the French word tromper, meaning "to deceive." First used in English in the 15th century, meaning fraud, deception, and an item or conduct of "worthless nonsense."

Should We Trust Tillerson?
– *The Baltimore Sun* with James Goodby; December 14, 2016

Donald Trump's nomination of ExxonMobil CEO Rex Tillerson to be the nation's next secretary of state — after a protracted consideration of candidates — suggests the president-elect understands the position must be filled by a person of character, depth and vision. Mr. Tillerson leads one of the world's largest multinational companies and is accustomed to working with foreign leaders and to running a large organization often described as a "quasi-state."

But his nomination also poses major challenges, especially in two critical respects. While clearly knowledgeable about energy, he has very limited familiarity with many complex issues ranging from nuclear weapons to numerous treaty relationships to decades-long conflicts, and there is little sign he knows much about China. Equally difficult, particularly in light of reports by the intelligence community that Russia intervened in the presidential election, are his very close relationship with Russian president Vladimir Putin and Exxon's billions in investments in Russia.

The Exxon executive criticized Western sanctions against Russia's military aggression in Crimea and Ukraine. He did so from a business perspective because Exxon struck a deal in 2011 with Russia that gave Exxon access to extensive Arctic resources. But what's good for Exxon is not necessarily what's good for America.

The nominee is bound to face rigorous grilling from senators in the wake of the CIA's conclusions about recent Russian cyberattacks against the U.S., which the intelligence agency says were intended to swing the election in Mr. Trump's favor. Republican leaders in Congress condemned the Russian intervention, and in a radio interview, Sen. John McCain, chairman of the Senate's Armed Services Committee, called Mr. Putin a "thug, a murderer, and a killer" and later added "butcher" to the list.

Leading European nations, America's closest allies, are bound to be concerned by Mr. Tillerson's nomination, especially after a campaign in which Mr. Trump questioned the importance of the North Atlantic Treaty Organization (NATO). Recently, Germany's leader Angela Merkel called for a toughening of those sanctions due to Russia's continuing lack of cooperation in Ukraine.

Mr. Tillerson's nomination could promote U.S. interests in important areas, however, notably in nuclear proliferation. Russia has backed away from nuclear negotiations in recent years, and improved ties may enable renewed cooperation. Despite Exxon's earlier skepticism regarding climate change and potential cover up of some risks associated with it, Mr. Tillerson has acknowledged that CO2 emissions have a warming effect on the planet, and he has supported a carbon tax.

The critical role played by a secretary of state has been demonstrated time and again in the nation's history. George Marshall led the recovery of Europe with the Marshall plan, Dean Acheson helped create NATO, and George Shultz worked alongside Ronald Reagan to achieve momentous arms control agreements.

The crucial role of the next secretary is magnified by Mr. Trump's total lack of experience in foreign policy and national security. Mr. Trump is a kind of blank slate — with views on important issues that range from sensible to bizarre.

A secretary of state is a president's senior foreign policy adviser and first among equals in the cabinet. He or she must be a strategic thinker with a deep grasp of the nation's interests and the need for broad public support.

Selection of a strong secretary is especially crucial to offset the heavy accent of military personnel already chosen for the cabinet. If confirmed, Mr. Tillerson will need to be a kind of balance wheel between two generals with starkly different views on key issues: Mr. Trump's choices for defense, Gen. James Mattis, and national security adviser, Lt. Gen. Michael Flynn.

General Mattis regards Russia as a serious threat to America's interests, whereas Lieutenant General Flynn appears friendly to Russia. General Mattis now defends President Barack Obama's nuclear agreement with Iran while Lieutenant General Flynn would tear it up. "Trump needs Cabinet officers willing to stand up to him and push back when he is wrong," noted Los Angeles Times columnist Doyle McManus. "Mattis has already done that."

In an interview in December's Foreign Service Journal, Mr. Shultz, a business executive himself before becoming Mr. Reagan's secretary of state, provides a candid assessment of the responsibility of the position. The coin of the realm is trust, Mr. Shultz said.

As a headstrong, tweet-prone leader, Donald Trump needs a smart, experienced and pragmatic secretary of state he can trust and who can help build confidence among the American people in Mr. Trump's wisdom and judgment. Will that be Mr. Tillerson?

Trump's First Crisis: North Korea's Nuclear Threat – *The Baltimore Sun* with James Goodby; January 3, 2017

Donald Trump unwisely picked a fight with China over Taiwan barely days after he eked out a victory in the 2016 election. Beyond embracing Vladimir Putin, his major foreign policy concerns during the campaign were defeating ISIS or revising the nuclear deal with Iran.

But the first real crisis of a Trump presidency is likely to come from the world's most isolated nation, North Korea. And the president-elect will soon learn that it is Chinese power and influence he will need to deal with North Korea and the threat posed by its nuclear weapons program.

The young and unpredictable leader of the Democratic Republic of North Korea, Kim Jong Un, declared last weekend that the country is approaching the final stage of an intercontinental ballistic rocket launch. In response, Mr. Trump tweeted late Monday that Mr. Kim's nuclear plans "won't happen!" and, an hour later, chided China for not helping "with North Korea."

Taking advantage of divisions between the United States and China over North Korea during the last decade or more, the "Hermit Kingdom" has continued to build a nuclear arsenal that already threatens its neighbors and will pose a threat to the United States in a few years if nothing is done to stop it.

Preemption is a possible response that will occur to some advisers to the new president, just as it did when China was in a comparable position in the 1960s. Cool heads prevailed then and should now, because a war and even a limited exchange of nuclear weapons on the Korean Peninsula would bring grave damage to our allies, South Korea and Japan, and cause global environmental damage.

The only plausible option is diplomacy. And a new administration in the capital of the world's most powerful nation should be clear-eyed enough to pick up where the Clinton administration left off with a review of U.S. policy and exploration of renewed negotiations.

For all of North Korea's intransigence, a decade and a half has been wasted during the administrations of both George W. Bush and Barack Obama. Scandal and shaky political leadership now hamper prospects of "sunshine" diplomacy from South Korea. And China, the one country with real leverage over North Korea, seems more worried about economic turmoil on its borders and immigration than the north's nuclear weapons.

Three recent expert reviews of North Korean policy underline the gravity of the situation — and conclude that time is running out for a peaceful resolution to one of the world's most serious problems.

A task force of the Council on Foreign Relations reported that North Korea's accelerating nuclear and missile progress poses "a grave and expanding threat" to the region, to U.S. allies and U.S. forces, and to the U.S. homeland.

Criticizing recent policies, the report urged a dual-track approach to engage North Korea, coordinating sanctions and deterrence with China while offering incentives to end the north's isolation and rush to expand its nuclear weapons arsenal. The CFR report urged renewed efforts to bring about a unified Korean peninsula.

A Hoover Institution-Johns Hopkins report urged revival of a search for common ground among northeast Asian nations similar to the one launched during the Clinton administration by former Secretary of Defense William J. Perry.

A recent conference of the Center for Strategic and International Studies in Washington D.C. drew similar conclusions. Leading experts agreed that a return to the so-called "six-party talks" was important, though unlikely. They concluded that without direct talks with China to deflect North Korea from its current path, a crisis is likely to develop in the near future. The U.S. and its allies must establish a "firm, but restrained" declaratory policy of consequences if North Korea were to proceed with its plans to place a nuclear weapon on a ballistic missile that could reach the U.S. mainland.

A formal treaty to end the 1950-1953 Korean War could serve as part of a policy framework for the incoming Trump administration if it can develop a broad-based agenda for negotiations among the leading powers in Northeast Asia. A narrow focus on North Korea's nuclear weapons program — one it clings to for legitimacy — has not been a formula for successful talks.

Unfortunately, there is no multilateral mechanism in Northeast Asia to promote peace and security. There is no mechanism to oversee implementation of agreements to get beyond the 1953 armistice. High-level meetings between North and South Korea have all but vanished. So, creating a network of nations to enable dialogue and negotiations will be a necessary first step to broader security agreements in the region.

If ever there was a time for "the art of the deal," this is it.

Compare the Most Inspiring Quotes from Past Presidents to Trump
– *The Dallas Morning News*; September 20, 2018

Presidential historians all have their favorite quotations of the 44 leaders of these United States of America. Here is my personal list of the most meaningful and memorable in the context of the grave political circumstances of the country in 2018. They touch on honesty, integrity, courage, character, freedom of speech, immigration and vision in international affairs.

George Washington: Paying tribute to his soldiers after the 1783 peace treaty in Paris to end the Revolution: "Happy, thrice happy, shall they be pronounced hereafter in erecting this stupendous fabric of freedom and empire on the broad basis of independence, and establishing an asylum for the poor and oppressed of all nations and religions." (April 18, 1783)

John Adams: "Facts are stubborn things, and whatever our wishes, our inclinations, or the dictates of our passion, they cannot alter the state of facts and evidence." (Boston massacre trials, December 1770)

Thomas Jefferson: "Were it left for me to decide whether we should have a government without newspapers, or newspapers without a government, I should not hesitate a moment to prefer the latter." (Jan. 18, 1787)

James Madison: Arguing for a strong Constitution, to prevent the "violence and damage caused by factions," Madison identified factions as "a number of citizens, whether a minority or a majority of the whole, who are united and actuated by some common impulse of passion or interest adverse to the rights of citizens or to the permanent and aggregate interests of the country." (Federalist Papers, Oct. 27, 1787)

John Quincy Adams: "Wherever the standard of freedom and independence has been unfurled, there will [America's] heart, her benedictions, her prayers, be. But she goes not abroad in search of monsters to destroy." (July 4, 1821)

Abraham Lincoln: "It is for us the living, rather, to be dedicated here to the unfinished work which they who fought here have thus far so nobly advanced. .... That this nation, under God, shall have a new birth of freedom and that government of the people, by the people, for the people, shall not perish from the earth." (Nov. 19, 1863, in Gettysburg).

Theodore Roosevelt: "Speak softly and carry a big stick."

Franklin D. Roosevelt: "This is pre-eminently the time to speak the truth, frankly and boldly. This great nation will endure as it has endured. [It is] my firm belief that the only thing we have to fear is fear itself — nameless, unreasoning, unjustified terror." (March 4, 1933; first inaugural address in the midst of the Depression)

Harry S. Truman: "If you can't stand the heat, get out of the kitchen." (1948)

Dwight D. Eisenhower: "In the councils of government, we must guard against the acquisition of unwarranted influence, whether sought or unsought, by the military-industrial complex. The potential for the disastrous rise of misplaced power exists, and will persist." (Jan. 17, 1961, final address)

John F. Kennedy: "And, so, my fellow Americans, ask not what your country can do for you; ask what you can do for your country." (Jan. 20, 1961, inaugural address)

Richard M. Nixon: "When a president does it that means that it's not illegal."

Ronald Reagan: (Speaking of signs of change in the Soviet Union): "Are these profound changes or token gestures? There is one sign that the Soviets can make that would be unmistakable, that would advance dramatically the cause of freedom and peace. General Secretary Gorbachev: If you seek peace and prosperity for the Soviet Union and for eastern Europe, come here to this gate. Mr. Gorbachev, Open this gate; tear down this wall." (June 12, 1987, Brandenburg Gate, West Berlin)

George H.W. Bush: "This is a victory for democracy and freedom, for the moral force of our values. ...[Mikhail Gorbachev's] legacy guarantees him an honored place in history and provides a solid basis for the United States to work in equally constructive ways with his successors." (Dec. 25, 1991, address to the nation upon the collapse of the Soviet Union, delivered without any sense of triumphalism.)

George W. Bush: "These acts of violence against innocents violate the fundamental tenets of the Islamic faith. Islam is peace. These terrorists don't represent peace; they represent evil and war. This is a great country. It is a great country because we share the same values of respect and dignity and human worth." (Sept. 17, 2001, speech to Islamic leaders in Washington)

Barack Obama: "The long sweep of America has been defined by forward motion, by a constant widening of our founding creed to embrace all and not just some." (2017 farewell address)

Donald J. Trump: "Why do we want all these people from [expletive] countries coming here?" (Jan. 18, 2018, at the White House)

Is it any wonder that the 170 scholars of the American Political Science Association, Democrat, Republican and independent, in rating the 44 men who have served as president for their integrity and effectiveness (there have been 45 presidencies, but only 44 presidents because Grover Cleveland served two non-consecutive terms) placed Mr. Trump at rock bottom? Trump displaced the previous cellar dweller, James Buchanan, whose ineptitude helped ignite the Civil War.

Part II. The Real "Enemy of the People;" First Signs of Incompetence

The most telltale image that foreshadowed the ultimate disaster of an administration led by Donald J. Trump was his very first cabinet meeting.

On June 12, 2017, Trump held that first full cabinet meeting – oddly five long months after his inauguration. With television cameras rolling, Trump went around the table and solicited statements from the officials. With one exception, every single person bestowed elaborate praise on Trump. If Trump had said "Jump," just about all of them looked like they'd hurl themselves out of their chairs.

Vice president Michael Pence talked about how it was "the greatest privilege of my life" to serve Trump. Nikki Haley, the new Ambassador to the United Nations, said Trump was restoring respect for the United States across the world, adding "We're back," as if the U.S. had just vanished.

Making the briefest statement, Secretary of Defense, Gen. James Mattis, simply said: "It is an honor to represent the men and women of the Department of Defense and we are grateful for the sacrifice our people are making….…"

There was one person with self-respect in the room.

It was a significant sign of times to come. With the exception of General Mattis, almost all of these cabinet members either have remained sycophantic supporters of Donald Trump, left under the shadow of corruption or quit because they disagreed with the president and had the courage to say so.

Many were out of office within a year – the beginnings of a chaotic ten-ring circus that has been the hallmark of the Trump administration. After eviscerating environmental regulations, EPA Secretary Scott Pruitt departed after numerous allegations of misuse of funds. Labor Secretary Tom Price – misuse of travel funds. Ryan Zinke, Interior secretary – questionable land deals.

More on matters of principle, Mattis and Secretary of State Tillerson left after collisions with Trump over his impulsive decision-making on critical foreign policy issues. Mattis quit after Trump, ignoring the advice of the general and other leaders, made reckless decisions on U.S. troops in Syria and a unilateral suspension of U.S. military exercises with South Korea to please North Korean dictator Kim Jung Un. Though Mattis denied saying it, Bob Woodward reported that Mattis said Trump had the brains of a fifth grader. Tillerson, who had expressed similar views, had already departed.

All of this dysfunction was playing out against a struggle by Trump to accomplish anything in his first 18 months in office. He did get to appoint two Supreme Court justices, hardly an achievement with a Republican Senate. But his attempt to throw out the Obama health care law collapsed when the late Sen. John McCain turned thumbs down.

Trump signed a tax cut bill that mainly enriched the top 1 % in the country and did virtually nothing for the so-called "base" of his supporters in lower-income ranks. It sent the deficit, a supposed GOP concern, through the roof. Other than that, he accomplished virtually nothing on critical

issues such as health care, infrastructure and immigration.
Despite repeated claims to "do something" after a series of
mass shootings, some by right-wing extremists inspired by
his rhetoric, he always backed off and took the line of the
National Rifle Association. He managed to agree with
Democrats on a criminal justice reform bill.

Meanwhile, several close Trump associates were headed for
jail and Trump himself was fending off more accusations of
adultery and sexual affairs. He proved to be more corrupt
than any recent president with continuing interest in his
hotels, profiting from federal use, and the venal behavior of
his children.

Other than his bizarre embrace of Russia and insulting
treatment of our allies, my main interest in Trump's first two
years revolved around his repeated condemnation of the
media, especially the print press, and his constant maligning
of professional civil servants – diplomats and intelligence
officers – as "the deep state."

Having spent 40 years in journalism and government, I
knew something about the media and government. I had
worked with many of the professional journalists, diplomats
and intelligence officers Trump was now demeaning as
"Nazis" and "fake news" purveyors.

Repeatedly, Trump showed his insecurity and thin-skinned
character by responding to the slightest criticism to blame
the press - even when the news they were reporting was 100
% accurate. Trump not only repeatedly scorned the work of
first-rate news organizations such as The New York Times,

the Washington Post and CNN, but it turned out he was a fan of right-wing types such as Rush Limbaugh and Alex Jones (who called the massacre of teachers and children at Sandy Hook a hoax).

Alarmingly, Trump continued to call the Times, Post and other major outlets "the enemy of the people" – a phrase popularized by Josef Stalin, the brutal dictator of the Soviet Union.

Beyond the chaos in the White House, his lack of accomplishment in domestic policy and near-total failure in foreign policy, the most damning and ironic proof of the disaster of Donald Trump, the man who promised to "drain the swamp," was that many of his closest associates – Michael Flynn, Paul Manafort, Michael Cohen – were all either in jail, had pleaded guilty or in prison.

Not surprisingly, when Trump attended a World Series game in Washington in the fall, 2019, the crowd chanted "Lock him up." Wincing, withdrawing to his seat, Donald John Trump did not dare go to another game. When the Nationals won the World Series, it meant the capitol had a champion – but not in the White House. There sat David McCullough's clown – with narcissistic ego, dyed orange hair and a fake tan to boot.

GOP Should Choose Country Before Party – *The Baltimore Sun* with James Goodby; February 5, 2017

A small number of Republican senators soon face a "profile in courage" challenge as President Donald Trump and his clique of advisers run roughshod over the U.S. Constitution, its guarantees and the national interest of the American people.

Through the recent ban on entry to the U.S. by refugees and many Muslims, the undermining of traditional American alliances, the continued insults on the nation's intelligence community (not to mention intelligence), and the effort to intimidate a free press, Mr. Trump and his acolytes are acting as if they have dictatorial power.

If these trends continue, moderate Republican senators, as many as 10, will have to put the country's interests ahead of party and say they cannot support radical, ill-conceived policies of isolationism, environmental degradation and severe cutbacks in domestic programs. Republicans hold a narrow 52-48 edge in the Senate, which must approve cabinet-level nominees, treaties and judicial appointments. No one has to switch parties, but a temporary alliance across party lines would halt the Trump machine in its tracks.

Two steps in particular could lead to a sharp confrontation with President Trump by a solid number of GOP senators —

possibly leading to a shift in the balance of power in the Senate against the president.

One is Mr. Trump's continued embrace of Vladimir Putin, a virtual dictator who has overseen the first aggression in Europe since the end of World War II, and the president's refusal to accept conclusive proof of Russian interference in our election.

The second, equally grave move by Mr. Trump was to remove the chairman of the Joint Chiefs of Staff from the key national security-focused Principals Committee, and add his ideological minder, Steve Bannon. That change in the National Security Council was sharply criticized by Sen. John McCain, an Arizona Republican, as a "radical departure" and by former Secretary of Defense Robert Gates as "a big mistake."

Many GOP senators are — in varying degrees — embarrassed, irritated, outraged or even disgusted by a number of Trump steps. A few condemned Mr. Trump during the campaign, including Susan Collins of Maine, Lisa Murkowski of Alaska, and Ben Sasse of Nebraska. Others sharply criticized him for his hateful rhetoric, sexual bravado and irresponsible positions on important issues such as nuclear proliferation and climate change.

The two most critical senators are the most respected members on national security: Senator McCain, who has labeled Mr. Putin a "butcher," a "murderer" and a "thug," and Lindsey Graham, of South Carolina. Both are angry at

Mr. Trump's dalliance with Mr. Putin and calling the NATO alliance obsolete.

There are any number of critical issues and opportunities in days ahead for these senators to confront Mr. Trump. And they could be joined by other independent voices — Rand Paul of Kentucky, Jeff Flake of Arizona, Marco Rubio of Florida — to set Mr. Trump and his cohort back on their heels.

A shot across the bow of the White House is badly needed — and soon. The most likely prospect of a tough note to Mr. Trump from his own party is the strong possibility that his nominee for education secretary, Betsy DeVos, will be rejected. Both Senators Collins and Murkowski have announced their opposition to her nomination; only one more GOP vote would sink it.

Another showdown could come on the confirmation vote on Sen. Jeff Sessions as attorney general — an ever more critical position in light of the hastily-conceived ban on Muslims and the firing of the acting attorney general. This week's arbitrary suspension of rules by the Judiciary Committee's Republican chairman to advance Trump nominations is a worrisome sign of an anti-democratic trend.

A clash could occur during review of the Supreme Court nominee, Judge Neil Gorsuch, or on a vital appropriation measure. One target could be the budget for the National Security Council, whose director, Michael Flynn, has been a key figure in the Trump administration's cozy ties with Putin's Russia.

John F. Kennedy wrote a memorable book about senators in American history who stood up for their beliefs and conscience — against the tide of opinion in their party or their state. He depicted actions by Republicans and Democrats, from John Quincy Adams to Robert Taft, who "were elected because [voters] had confidence in our judgment to determine the best interests of the nation." The title was "Profiles in Courage."

A new chapter to this volume, perhaps an entirely expanded edition, needs to be written. Today's Republicans and Democrats need to come together to stand up for American values, including the independence of our legal system, and the basic tenets of a bipartisan foreign policy that has underpinned the world order ever since World War II.

Trump is Failing in His Global Responsibility to Control Nuclear Weapons
– *The Dallas Morning News* with James Goodby; February 20, 2017

Threaten war with Iran. Challenge China's most sensitive national security concern, Taiwan, then recant. Spread doubt among our most important allies that the United States stands with them for democracy and the rule of law. All in three Twitter-filled weeks.

And, on top of that, continue to embrace Russia and its authoritarian leader, Vladimir Putin, who has intervened militarily in Crimea and Ukraine and supported cyberattacks against the American electoral system. All of these steps add up to a reckless series of acts from the new leader of the most powerful country in the world, one so many countries look to for leadership and commitment to the rule of law, not to mention stability.

But President Donald Trump has failed in an even more critical aspect of the role of commander-in-chief. He has shown himself to be woefully lacking in understanding of his responsibility for the control of nuclear weapons.

Trump denounced the landmark 2011 New START (Strategic Arms Reduction Treaty) agreement in his first telephone call to Putin, according to the Reuters news agency. Trump reportedly said the updated and strengthened treaty was one of several bad deals negotiated by President Barack Obama. He showed little knowledge of the treaty during the phone call.

Trump showed a complete lack of understanding of the treaty during the election campaign. He said it allowed Russia to increase its nuclear weapons inventory, and he charged, erroneously, that the U.S. was not permitted to do so for nondeployed weapons.

The New START agreement has advanced U.S., Russian and global interests by lowering and capping the two nations' strategic nuclear arsenals. Daryl Kimball, director of the Arms Control Association, said, "Mr. Trump appears to be totally clueless about this nuclear risk reduction treaty and the unique dangers of nuclear weapons."

This episode, the lies and resignation of Michael Flynn as national security adviser, and the careless discussions of the sensitive North Korean missile launch in a wide-open restaurant last weekend underline the frightful disarray at the top levels of the Trump administration, especially in the area of national security.

Not surprisingly, Putin appears to have chosen this moment of chaos in the Trump administration to deploy ground-based cruise missiles in a glaring violation of one of the key nuclear arms treaties of the post-Cold War period. The decision effectively tears up the 1987 agreement to eliminate intermediate-range nuclear forces that threatened NATO countries. While the deployment was in planning stages during the end of the Obama presidency, confirmation of the move has still not drawn any criticism from the Trump administration.

President Harry Truman, Obama and every president in between understood the threat that nuclear weapons pose to our existence and to all life on this planet.

Presidents Dwight Eisenhower and John Kennedy worked to ban nuclear tests that had been adding radioactivity to the Earth's atmosphere. President Lyndon Johnson negotiated a treaty that limited the spread of nuclear weaponry to many potential nuclear nations. Richard Nixon, Ronald Reagan, and George H.W. Bush concluded landmark nuclear treaties with Moscow that changed the course of history, including treaties to reduce the number of strategic nuclear weapons on land and sea-based missiles and nuclear-capable bombers.

President George W. Bush concluded with Putin a treaty that reduced deployed U.S. and Russian nuclear warheads. Presidents since 1992 have engaged American expertise and resources to tighten controls over fissile material anywhere in the world where terrorists could acquire it. Obama followed in this tradition, reaching agreement with Putin on the New START, which gives both countries until 2018 to reduce deployed nuclear weapons to 1,550 each, the lowest in decades. Obama initiated four global summit meetings designed to improve controls over proliferation of fissile material.

While Trump's embrace of Putin has alarmed so many people in this country, Europe and around the world, especially his implicit approval of Russian aggression, there is an urgent need for renewed cooperation to reduce nuclear stockpiles. But that diplomacy has to begin with a clear, no-nonsense policy toward Russia on all issues, and, above all, on nuclear weapons.

Lack of knowledge and casual remarks about such awesome responsibilities and weapons that could kill millions and destroy the Earth are dangerous.

All presidents in the nuclear age have understood this. Reagan put it well when he said in his 1984 State of the

Union address: "A nuclear war cannot be won and must never be fought."

As commander-in-chief, Donald Trump clearly has a lot of homework to do. Let's pray he can get away from his Twitter account and do it.

Comey Testimony Solves Second Biggest Mystery of the 2016 Election
– *The Dallas Morning News*; **March 22, 2017**

The second greatest surprise of the 2016 election has now become clear: Why FBI Director James Comey released information about the potentially compromising emails of an aide to Hillary Clinton nine days before the election.

The No. 1 surprise, of course, remains Donald Trump's victory. The clues to that have emerged in a number of scenarios ranging from the Democratic party miscalculations and over-confidence to a listless campaign by Clinton herself.

My own conclusion rests on three factors: apathy, an ill-informed electorate and prejudice. Apathy in the low turnout among millennials and minorities; ill-informed voters hoodwinked into thinking that a rich TV-reality star would really help them; and prejudice, dislike of the first black president and female candidate mixed with Trump's

racist rhetoric about immigration, Muslims and Mexican
"rapists."

But the mystery of Comey's 11th-hour intervention now falls
into place with his testimony Monday in which he not only
confirmed that the investigation into possible Russian
collusion with the Trump campaign goes back to July 2016,
and the allegations are very serious, but also that Trump's
charge that Obama tapped his phones at Trump Tower is
baseless.

It all comes down to a combination of credibility and
erroneous polls.

Put yourself in Comey's shoes last fall, two weeks or so
before election day. A respected civil servant, a Republican
who had stood up for the rule of law against intense political
pressure during the George W. Bush administration, Comey
was confronted with seemingly important evidence of
additional misuse of email servers by a close aide to Hillary
Clinton.

While criticizing the former secretary of state before
Congress after an initial investigation of her misuse of an
email server, but concluding that there was no basis for
criminal action, Comey had promised to return to Capitol
Hill if any further evidence came to light. Then there was
new evidence, produced, it is alleged, by FBI staffers who
were close to former New York mayor Rudy Giuliani, a
fervent Trump backer. While still uncertain, several of those
agents were said to have threatened to leak the evidence

against Clinton's aide if Comey did not report it to key members of Congress.

Also consider the circumstances at the time. Virtually all polls, even the most accurate in prior elections, predicted Clinton was going to win by a large margin.

If you can add two and two, you have the answer to why Comey reported that additional information to members of Congress just before election day, and it was promptly released by GOP members. The fact that a quick examination of the emails concluded there were no issues days before the election is immaterial.

Two and two: to Comey, his credibility was at stake. It is clear now that just before the election he knew how serious the evidence of Russian intervention had been, but both the intelligence community and the FBI had not completed a thorough investigation. So, faced with a choice of holding back information or having it leaked by others in his office, he decided to make it available.

It is impossible to know if he had any personal interest in the outcome of the election. But it is not a stretch to conclude that he decided such a release would 1) keep his commitment to report new information, 2) take a step that probably wouldn't affect the outcome of the election, and 3) retain his credibility as an independent law enforcement official. That independence would be all the more critical if the probe of Russian interference proved to border on criminal activity or treason. As it clearly does.

No one should now wonder why Trump was so furious when he discovered that newly confirmed Attorney General Jeff Sessions had recused himself from any investigation into Russian involvement after being caught lying about his meetings with the Russian ambassador. Sessions, Comey's boss, was Trump's last best hope of shutting down the investigation that now looks likely to get to the bottom of Trump's truly bizarre embrace of Russian behavior and its leader Vladimir Putin.

The FBI director stood tall in an extraordinary session, defending our rule of law: "When there is an effort by a foreign nation-state to mess with that, to destroy that, to corrupt that, it is very serious."

Kelly Brings Integrity to the White House, but How Will That Play?
– *The Dallas Morning News* with Col. Sam Gardiner; August 8, 2017

By all counts, the appointment of Gen. John Kelly as White House chief of staff holds out the prospect of a badly needed turnaround to end the chaos, confusion and duplicity emanating from President Donald Trump and his administration.

The abrupt dismissal of the foul-mouthed Anthony Scaramucci and other initial steps Kelly has taken suggest that he may be able to bring the kind of discipline and order demanded of — and now completely absent from — the highest office in the land.

But unless Trump does an about-face in his own manners and stops with the off-the-cuff tweeting and lying, Kelly may not last any longer than Reince Priebus, the president's first chief of staff. And it won't be Kelly's fault at all.

Kelly's honesty and calm demeanor not only happen to reflect his character. They also constitute an all-embracing compass of his life and career as an outstanding military officer, as a member of the U.S. Marine Corps for 40 years.

To never lie and ... to abide by an uncompromising code of integrity. Those words are from the first paragraph of the Marine Code.

Trump obviously does not have the same compass. He would even lie about a call from the head of the Boy Scouts. He would lie about a phone call from the president of Mexico. His early ambition to be president is widely seen to have been based on a lie: that President Barack Obama was not a U.S. citizen.

In short, Kelly is going to be a problem for Trump, and Trump is going to be a problem for Kelly.

Not only is truthfulness part of his code, but Kelly also could face a court-martial if he were to lie. As a retired officer, he remains subject to the Uniform Code of Military Justice.

One has to believe Trump was not aware he would be working so closely with someone governed by this. A person subject to the Uniform Code of Military Justice who, "with intent to deceive, signs any false record, return, regulation, order, or other official document, knowing it to be false, or makes any other false official statement knowing it to be false, shall be punished as a court-martial may direct."

Knowing this, as the general does even if the president does not, Kelly may be obliged to keep a lower profile in the White House than one might expect. There's nothing wrong with that tack, especially if he can rescue the president and his staff from the conflicting and confusing lines of responsibility and access.

Thus, Kelly may well stay away from news conferences and public appearances where he could be asked if a particular statement or decision of the president's is true.

Faced with a direct question about the truthfulness of a statement by Trump, it will not be enough for Kelly to answer the question and later say, "I misspoke," as President Ronald Reagan's spokesman, Larry Speakes, once apologized.

In the first six months of the Trump presidency, a number of high-level confidants have been caught lying, including Donald Trump Jr. about his secretive meetings with Russians, and retired Gen. Michael Flynn, the president's first national security adviser. He told falsehoods to Vice President Mike Pence and failed to report foreign payments in required reports for international travel.

It is a crucial question. How can other world leaders be viewing the U.S., especially if an international crisis were to occur, when they cannot trust what the president says? Not comfortably, when a president constantly speaks negatively about women and Muslims, about the U.S. Constitution and the rights of a free press, and repeatedly tells baldfaced lies.

Another Marine Corps officer, decorated Vietnam veteran Robert Mueller, offered a stirring reminder of the importance of truthfulness and integrity this spring in a commencement address at Tabor Academy in Marion, Mass.

Shortly after his appointment as a special counsel to investigate possible collusion between the Trump campaign and Russian officials, Mueller, the former FBI director, told graduates that one must never sacrifice his or her integrity. Without mentioning Trump or the inquiry, Mueller observed:

"You can be smart, aggressive, articulate, but if you are not honest, your reputation will suffer, and once lost, a good reputation can never, ever be regained." Then, quoting Eric Groeschel, Mueller concluded: "If you don't have integrity, nothing else matters. If you do have integrity, nothing else matters."

<u>**The GOP Created this Trump Mess and Here's How They Could Clean it Up**</u>
<u>**– *The Dallas Morning News*; August 24, 2017**</u>

Tennessee Senator Bob Corker's harsh critique of Donald Trump's lack of competence and stability has opened the door for all moderate Republicans to break ranks with this clearly unqualified president.

But it is past time for moderate Republicans to do much more than criticize Trump. Due to the primary responsibility of the GOP for the nearly decades-long dysfunction in Congress, an ideologically extreme campaign that paved the way for Trump to gain the presidency, GOP leaders must now act.

One Republican after another has turned against Trump as a result of his repeated demonstrations of poor judgment, off-the-cuff insults and lies, lack of understanding of the importance of his office, and now openly racist remarks in defending people who admire Adolf Hitler and the Ku Klux Klan.

GOP leaders in Congress crossed their fingers and prayed that the candidate who ridiculed Muslims and Mexicans and joked about assaulting women would rise to the challenge of the presidency and become an effective leader. They mistakenly thought they could control him and pass their agenda.

Instead, one day after another for seven months we've seen a crude and narcissistic man prove that he has no concept of leadership, little regard for the Constitution (condemning a free press, demonizing religious groups), and scant respect for his own government (failing to work with his own party to pass legislation, referring to members of the intelligence community as Nazis).

In foreign policy, ignoring capable advisers, he has inflamed grave international issues with early-morning tweets and advocated policies on nuclear weapons, trade and climate change that hurt America's long-term interests and isolate the country from our closest allies. Apparently indebted to Russian help to win the election, he has failed to appreciate the threat posed by Russian aggression in eastern Europe and repeatedly praised its leader, Vladimir Putin.

One of the most experienced and respected men in America, James Clapper, the former director of intelligence who served 10 presidents, this week described Trump as "downright scary and disturbing, a complete intellectual, moral and ethical void" who should not be trusted with the nuclear codes. Trump, he said in an interview with CNN, is "unfit" for office.

What can be done? Three practical, plausible steps could remove him from the White House.

1. The investigation into possible collusion between Russian interests and the Trump campaign. This may lead to charges ranging from obstruction of justice to tax evasion to

conspiracy. It is still impossible to know if Trump himself or close aides and relatives will be accused of any crimes.

By most legal opinions, impeachment is the only constitutional avenue to charges against a sitting president. That scenario could be lengthy.

2. The 25th amendment. It was passed after the assassination of John F. Kennedy to clarify succession in the event not only of death or grave illness but also "an inability to discharge the powers and duties" of the office. It requires a cumbersome group to agree, including a vice-president, members of a president's cabinet and Congress.

3. A rump GOP caucus in Congress. Why shouldn't senators such as Jeff Flake and John McCain of Arizona, Lindsey Graham of South Carolina, Susan Collins of Maine, Lisa Murkowski of Alaska, who were all ridiculed by the president, get together and form an independent caucus outside the party until Trump acts more presidential or leaves office?

These senators were not the main culprits in the disastrous, un-American turn of the Republican party under the leadership of Kentucky's Mitch McConnell. But they went along. It is now up to them to repay the country for the course of events that has ensued, one that has placed the country, as Senator Corker said, "in great peril."

In March 2016, Norman Ornstein of the conservative American Enterprise Institute and Thomas Mann of the

Brookings Institution provided this damning assessment of the Republican party:

"The Republican party has become an insurgent outlier — ideologically extreme, contemptuous of an inherited social and economic regime, scornful of compromise, unpersuaded by conventional understanding of facts, evidence and science, and dismissive of its political opposition."

They stood by their assessment in 2016. Basically forecasting the rise of Trump, they concluded: "It is a self-inflicted wound, but one with disastrous consequences for us all."

There is a fourth option. And that is for Donald J. Trump to recognize that his lack of experience, sense of history, commitment to America's leading role in the world, or any moral and ethical compass, compel him to resign.

The flag of the Native American, or Know Nothing party of the mid-19th century.

<u>Trump is Reviving the Nativist 19th Century Political Party, the Know Nothings
– *The Dallas Morning News*; November 12, 2017</u>

It was first called the Order of United Americans. Then it was renamed the Order of the Star-Spangled Banner. Then it became the Native American Party. And that was shortened to the American Party.

Its popular name, derived from its origin as a secret society, was the Know Nothings. That stemmed from the anti-Catholic, anti-immigrant obsession of the party, its habits of passwords and hand signs, and the commitment of its members, if asked their political allegiance, to say: "I know nothing."

For nearly 20 years, the Know Nothings were a major third party in the United States in the mid-19th century, and generally a mean, destructive force.

They faded as the 1860 election neared. Slavery overtook immigration as the primary issue of the day and a little-known but courageous Illinois lawyer by the name of Abraham Lincoln pulled the Republican Party together.

That was all long ago, in the 1840s and 1850s.

Guess what? The Know Nothings are making a comeback in the early 21st century, largely as a result of the phenomenon of Donald J. Trump and his hateful, nativist behavior. And with open warfare now declared in the Republican Party, between traditional conservatives and a right-wing faction that wants to isolate the United States in world affairs, throw up walls against all immigrants, exalt racism and turn back the clock on social matters, there is a clear risk that the party of Lincoln could be split apart by the 21st century version of the Know Nothings.

Trump — master of the big lie and gratuitous insults — outdid himself recently when he boasted of "great unity" in the GOP, not long after a respected Republican senator condemned him as reckless and immoral, another leading GOP senator described him as a child needing day care, and his own secretary of state called him a "moron." Trump bragged about "great unity" after the last Republican president accused him of dividing the country with bigoted behavior, and Trump's chief strategist outlined plans to attack traditional Republicans, including majority leader Mitch McConnell.

Trump, now with the lowest approval ratings of any recent president in his first year, is losing his marbles if he sees "great unity" in the GOP.

Coincidentally, one of the most reliable political analysis companies, Pew Research, just released a comprehensive report on an increasingly polarized country.

The report documented the growing and bitter divide in the Republican Party. It described "core" and "new-era" Republicans as backers of traditional values and American leadership in the world, more accepting of immigration and changing social norms such as same-sex marriage. It showed how "country first" and "market skeptic" factions, basically older, less educated citizens, are more hostile to a global role, opposed to social change and inclined to back Trumpian policies right or wrong.

Noting such cleavages in the GOP, a respected columnist recently concluded that the party of Lincoln is becoming the party of Trump. Maybe in the short term; it is more likely that the party is on its way to becoming the party of the Know Nothings. The evidence is clear.

One, Trump and his supporters mimic the hateful rhetoric and actions of the largely white, Protestant members of the 19th century Know Nothings who torched churches, instigated riots and even elected 100 members of Congress at one point in their blind opposition to immigration, then largely from Ireland and Germany.

Two, Trump and his supporters show the same disdain for science and the future by withdrawing from the climate change accord and dismantling entire institutions such as the State Department and the Environmental Protection Agency designed to assure diplomatic engagement and promote public health. Despite overwhelming evidence that climate change stems in part from human activity, this president knows nothing. Climate change is a "Chinese hoax."

Three, on economic policy, Trump is pursuing "beautiful tax cut" legislation that benefits mainly corporations and the wealthiest 1 percent, increases middle-class taxes and will raise the national deficit by $1.5 trillion. In a new book, The Truth Matters, Republican economist Bruce Bartlett describes GOP glorification of tax cuts as "total mythology" and its "trickle down" approach as "complete nonsense."

Lastly, on foreign policy, Trump and his cohort, including his alter-ego, Steve Bannon, support isolationism, a disastrous policy of the 1930s GOP that emboldened Nazi Germany and Japan to initiate World War II. Sen. John McCain, R.-Ariz., describes Trump's foreign policy as "half-baked, spurious nationalism."

While the U.S. did not have an international standing at the time of the original Know Nothings, we do now. The U.S. has been a leader of the democratic free world — until Trump. Asked his view of Russian intervention in the 2016 election, confirmed by all American intelligence agencies, Trump has said: "I know nothing [about Russia.]"

Trump's Reckless Rhetoric is Fueling a Climate of Hate
– *Bangor Daily News*; October 29, 2018

Hillary Clinton committed a grave error in the 2016 presidential election with her reference to many Americans as "deplorables." Yet ever since his narrow, Russian-aided win in that election, Donald Trump has proved himself to be the ultimate deplorable.

Instead of being a serious, professional commander in chief, one who leads and seeks to unite the country, President Trump bears major responsibility for the climate of hate and divisiveness that has given rise to the violent attacks in Pittsburgh and across the country.

The mass shooting at a Jewish synagogue in Pittsburgh and the mail-bomb attack against Democratic leaders have been encouraged and fueled by Trump's inflammatory rhetoric and loud attacks on minorities, immigrants, the press and basically almost any person who criticizes him and his policies.

On Wednesday after the bomb plot was foiled, Trump declared that "threats of political violence have no place in the United States." Going ahead with political rallies in the midst of these tragedies, Trump appealed for "civility" in our political discourse.

Well, to identify a prime cause of the deplorable lack of civility and the rise in hate speech, demonization of minorities and callous disregard for constitutional protections of free speech and the press, the president has no farther to look than straight into the mirror in the White House. Trump is more responsible than any other single person for creating a climate of fear, hate and potential violence.

From his rallies and vilification of Clinton, encouraging "lock her up" jeers, to constantly pointing out journalists and critics as "horrible" people, Trump has energized the radical right — many of whom endorse violence. He continues to shred the Constitution and demean professional government employees of the FBI and CIA, whom he has called "Nazis."

Fact: It was Trump who encouraged supporters at his campaign rallies to go after anyone who heckled him. After the murder of Saudi journalist Jamal Khashoggi, Trump praised a Montana politician for "body-slamming" a reporter.

Fact: Trump has regularly called hard-working members of the press "enemies of the people" — a pejorative often employed by Joseph Stalin, the dictator of the Soviet Union.

Fact: It was Trump who cavalierly remarked that there was blame on both sides after a neo-Nazi rally in Charlottesville,

Virginia, led to violence and the death of an innocent young woman.

It has been the president of the United States who day in, day out employs demeaning, often racist and foul-mouthed remarks about women, Muslims, African-American professional athletes who express free speech and Mexican or other immigrants.

Trump cannot have it both ways. Instead of inciting fear and stoking tension, a president should be serving as a high-minded leader, seeking to unify the country. Instead, he remains in campaign mode, spending more time at rallies that inflate his ego than he does in Washington trying to improve the condition of the country and address serious international problems. Sadly, most Republicans look the other way.

Hate crimes in the United States have escalated sharply since Trump took office, with a California State University study finding hate crimes rose 12 percent in 2017 over 2016 levels. A lead researcher said a prime cause can be "public figures who demonize vulnerable populations."

Studies also show an alarming rise in anti-Semitic attacks and abuse throughout the country in recent years.

Two respected Americans, historian Jon Meacham and former John McCain aide Steve Schmidt, have said the attempted bomb attacks on Democratic leaders constitute the worst act of violence in America since the assassination of Abraham Lincoln.

At a far more difficult moment in American history, as the Great Depression gripped America and millions of people lost their jobs and stood in line for bread, President Franklin D. Roosevelt gave an inspiring address on his inauguration in 1933.

"This is pre-eminently time to speak the truth … This great nation will endure as it has endured … So, first of all, let me assert my firm belief that the only thing we have to fear is fear itself — nameless, unreasoning, unjustified terror."

In the fall of 2018, it is time to speak another grim truth. Perhaps the main thing we have to fear today is Trump and his reckless, inflammatory and incompetent behavior.

Part III. From Russia with Love

Strangely, in 2016, a Republican candidate for the presidency of the United States deeply admired a once little-known Russian spy, Vladimir Vladimirovich Putin, who had come to power in the chaotic aftermath of the collapse of the Soviet Union.

Donald John Trump's infatuation was all the more remarkable in light of the fact that his early mentor was Roy Cohn, the consigliere to Joseph McCarthy, the rabidly anti-Communist and eventually discredited senator. Now the would-be President of the United States was an admirer of Russia, a nation marked as an outright foe of the U.S. in the Trump administration's and other National Security Strategy documents.

During the campaign, Trump had gone out of his way to praise Putin, a man determined to undermine American and western democracy and alliances. Putin, he praised, was a more effective leader than Barack Obama. But there was much more to learn about Trump's relations with Moscow – before and after Trump's election.

Under pressure from the Trump campaign, then headed by the later convict Paul Manafort, the GOP toned down criticism of Russian intervention in Ukraine in the platform for the party convention.

But it was not until I read a series of articles by Craig Ungar in *The New Republic* that I began to understand the depth of Trump's indebtedness to Russia. Millions of dollars had flowed into Trump hotels and apartments from the Russia mafia and a small but wealthy clan of oligarchs who had reaped billions from the collapse of the Soviet Union.

The flow of money from Russia began as early as the mid-1980s as these shrewd operators anticipated the weakening stability of the USSR and began buying apartments in New York – many in Trump Tower. Ungar's articles, later published in *House of Putin, House of Trump*, documented the large-scale laundering of dirty capital, much of it from friends of Putin.

Eric Trump admitted that Russian investments saved Trump businesses during the 2007-2008 financial meltdown. "We don't rely on American banks. We have all the funding we need from Russia."

In his term in office, Donald Trump has repeatedly expressed his affection for Putin, tried to restore Russia to membership in the G-7 and sought to block or limit imposition of sanctions on Russia for its brutal intervention in Ukraine. One appalling incident in May, 2017 not only indicated his lack of experience but a readiness to favor Russia when he shared highly classified information about ISIS with Russia's foreign minister. Israeli leaders, whose intelligence agents were endangered by Trump's indiscretions, were outraged.

(Note #2.)

But my suspicion of Trump's willingness to place Russian interests ahead of U.S. national interests was not confirmed until the appalling spectacle at Helsinki in June, 2018 when an American president basically knelt down and kissed the feet of Vladimir Putin by saying that he accepted Putin's word that Russia did not interfere in the 2016 election – effectively dismissing the unanimous conclusion of all American intelligence agencies.

Trump's remarks were met by a torrent of abuse at home and around the world – except from shrinking cowards in the Republican party. One notable GOP exception was the late Sen. John McCain.

Trump's actions, McCain said, amounted to "one of the most disgraceful performances by an American president." Trump "abased himself abjectly,…. before a tyrant."

Intelligence reports of massive Russian interference in the 2016 election on Trump's behalf led to the appointment of a special counsel, Robert Mueller. After a long investigation, the Special Counsel's report concluded that there was a massive intervention by the Russians, on Trump's behalf, mostly through cyber-attacks meant to divide Americans and lower turnout. While it found no direct evidence of "collusion" between the Trump campaign and Russians, it concluded there was significant evidence that Trump obstructed justice in trying to block the investigation. It punted on a final judgment because of existing practice that a sitting president cannot be indicted.

Trump and his loyal Attorney General, William Barr seized the latter ambiguity to declare "all clear" and "exonerated" from "the Russian witch hunt" – which, of course, to any literate person, was far from the truth.

Trump's affection for Russia was also confirmed during the impeachment trial. He and his minions like Rudy Giuliani constantly sought to divert blame by claims that it was Ukraine, not Russia, that interfered in the 2016 election. Many professional diplomats and intelligence officers demolished that falsehood. The most succinct was Fiona Hill, a respected expert on Russia *in the administration.*

"Some of you (Republicans)," Hill said, seem to believe that it was Ukraine that interfered. "This is a fictional narrative perpetrated and propagated by the Russian security services themselves. The unfortunate truth is that Russia was the foreign power that systematically attacked our democratic institutions." Yet, every GOP senator, except Mitt Romney, placed Russian interests ahead of the U.S. constitution, the rule of law and our democratic values in voting to clear their "leader."

In April, 2020, Republican and Democratic members of the Senate Intelligence Committee approved – *unanimously* – a report that confirmed massive Russian interference in the 2016 election.

Amazingly, Trump has not made much of an effort to disprove his embrace of Russia and Putin, though multiple causes are likely – from the 2016 interference to the millions of rubles/dollars invested in Trump properties to fear of embarrassing Russian *kompromat* on his dealings with Russia. At the end of June, 2020, Trump was found to have ignored hard intelligence that Russia paid bounty money to the Taliban in Afghanistan to kill American soldiers – dating as far back as mid-2019.

One of the great unknowns remains Trump's income taxes. He has refused to release them as have other presidents. I am willing to bet that when they do come to light, they will reveal one of three features of Donald John Trump. One, that he is not so wealthy; two, that he is a skinflint (suggested by his payment of a $2 million fine for his foundation's diversion of donations from veterans to his political campaign) and three, he is heavily indebted to Russian interests. It could well be all three.

Here are several columns on an American president's bizarre – and anti-American - embrace of a foreign power that the official National Strategy of the United States identifies as a ruthless foe that seeks to undermine American democracy and our alliances.

'Here's my man;' U.S. President Donald Trump and Russia's President Vladimir Putin, at Helsinki, Finland, July 16, 2018.

Credit: Photo by Mikhail Metzel/TASS/Abaca Press

ARTICLES

Donald Trump: Russia's Biggest Fan
– *The Baltimore Sun;* June 16, 2018

Donald J. Trump is a Russian agent. What else can any sane and objective person conclude after his blindly pro-Russian — and anti-American — comment that Russia should be invited back into the G-7?

The dean of the Russian State University in Moscow observed that Mr. Trump took a "sledgehammer" to the G-7 and western alliances with his statement and that Vladimir Putin doesn't have to do anything: "Trump is doing it for him."

Mr. Trump, who brags that he does not read, is proving to be not only master of the big lie but ignorant of history and reality. Here are facts, not "fake news."

Fact: Russia was ejected in 2014 from what was then the G-8, the exclusive club of leading democratic countries, for sound strategic and moral reasons: Under its authoritarian ruler Vladimir Putin, Russia seized Crimea and invaded eastern Ukraine. Those forces are still there fighting to destabilize an independent nation.

These two acts were the most blatant cases of aggression in Europe since World War II.

Fact: Russian forces shot down a Malaysian airliner in 2014, killing all 298 passengers and crew, according to prosecutors in the Netherlands. An American, Quinn Lucas Schansman, a dual-national student from Indiana, was a passenger. Based on population, the 189 Dutch citizens killed are roughly proportional to the number of people killed in the 9/11 bombings of the World Trade Center. Russian officials, of course, blame others.

Fact: All American intelligence agencies concluded that Russia intervened with full-force cyberattacks and abuse of millions of social media websites to disrupt the 2016 presidential election, in which Mr. Trump eked out a narrow electoral victory. Russia has conducted similar cyberattacks in western European democracies.

And despite warnings of continuing meddling in the once-sacred American election system, the Trump administration has done nothing to protect it from Russian intervention in upcoming elections. In fact, Mr. Trump has tried to block or watered down tough sanctions against Russia, passed almost unanimously by Congress, for its intervention in the election. Mr. Trump also continues to lavish praise on Mr. Putin and sharply criticize our closest allies.

Fact: Billions of dollars have poured into Trump hotels and realty since the financial meltdown of 2007, when Donald Trump Jr. admits they were desperate for cash. Russian oligarchs have been caught red-handed shoveling millions to Mr. Trump's lawyer, Michael Cohen. Thirteen Russians have been indicted in the special counsel's investigation into the Russian election intervention.

Fact: Many Russian dissidents who have had the courage to speak up and oppose Mr. Putin's autocratic rule have been murdered or arbitrarily jailed, including respected political figures and journalists who were investigating Kremlin misrule and corruption. A former Russian intelligence agent was poisoned this year - by Russian agents, according to British authorities.

Fact: The annual National Security Strategy describes Russia as a major threat to the interests and values of the U.S.

One can go on and on with hard facts that place Russia as a serious hazard to not only the United States but an international order in which democratic processes, human rights and respect for the rule of law are uppermost. Even some Republicans recognized Mr. Trump's selective blindness when it comes to Russia. Sen. Ben Sasse of Nebraska said "Putin is not our friend. He is a thug using Soviet-style aggression to wage a shadow war against America."

It's true that there are legitimate reasons to want to improve relations with Russia — for American, European and global interests. Russia holds significant energy reserves, in addition to its vast nuclear arsenal (which Mr. Putin is attempting to strengthen despite no increased threat).

But Russia's economic throw-weight needs to be kept in perspective. Russia's economy, basically a one-note band that Mr. Putin has failed to diversify in two decades of rule, is ranked 13th in the world in terms of gross national product. The state of California's economy is 5th largest — two times the size of Russia's.

A new book by respected Russian author Masha Gessen, "The Future is History; How Totalitarianism Reclaimed Russia," outlines how many average citizens in Russia have had their hopes and dreams crushed by the return of the old

Soviet order in the form of a new "and unstoppable mafia state" under Mr. Putin.

But then again, maybe that's a plus in Mr. Trump's eyes.

Explaining Russia to Trump
– *The Dallas Morning News*; August 1, 2017

Imagine: Before President Trump signed the new sanctions against Russia passed overwhelmingly by Congress, the president (POTUS) sat down with his national security adviser to discuss a little history. Here is a possible conversation, not an actual accounting, but a tongue-in-cheek version of what just might have transpired.

"Tell me," says POTUS. "If Hillary Clinton could try to reset relations with Russia — even though she failed — bad Hillary — why can't I?"

"Well, Mr. President, Russia under Putin has done a lot of very bad things since relations with the United States went south."

"Okay, tell me," says POTUS. "When did they start going south? Under Clinton, Bill? That womanizer, bad person, very bad."

"Well, yes and no," replies the national security adviser. "Both he and Bush the Second, made some mistakes. Clinton tried to help Russia when Yeltsin was the president, but the vodka got Yeltsin, and Clinton and 43 pushed NATO expansion too hard."

"I knew it," says POTUS. "That NATO's at the root of all our problems with Russia."

"Ah, not quite, sir. NATO is the most successful alliance in modern times. It has held Western Europe and the United States together for 70 years and prevented the Soviet Union from expanding its communist empire. Even Nixon was against the Soviet Union. It collapsed in 1990-91, you'll recall."

"I was busy building all those casinos and hotels then. I wasn't paying a lot of attention to world affairs. Too many bad, very bad, immigrant workers to deal with."

The national security adviser then listed provocative actions by Vladimir Putin in the last five years, including his intervention in Ukraine and lack of cooperation on nuclear arms treaties, leading President Barack Obama and his Secretary of State, Hillary Clinton, to decide they could not work with him. And Putin's decision that he couldn't work with them.

"I knew it. It's all Clinton's fault. That's why I like Putin; he hates Hillary."

The national security adviser then recounted Russian misdeeds: seizure of Crimea, Russian troops destabilizing Ukraine, Russian bombers flying across the Baltic states. He briefly mentioned Russian interference in the 2016 U.S. election.

"Gee, that's bad, isn't it," replies POTUS. "During the campaign I was asked about Crimea; I thought it was part of Russia."

"You did miss that one, Mr. President."

"Now watch out, mister. I knew what I was doing, even if I wasn't up on all that foreign stuff. My base didn't care about the Russkies. What else should I know about?"

"Well, you know, don't you, that Putin rigs elections and controls the media, locks up people who challenge him? And some of them get shot or poisoned mysteriously?"

"Right!" exclaims POTUS. "He told me his poll ratings are in the 80s because he throttles the fake press. That's what I need to do."

The NSC adviser ignores the tangent. "To be honest, sir, you really need a full, clear picture of Russia today. You know it's not really that powerful a country, don't you?"

"What do you mean? They have all those nuclear weapons," says POTUS.

"Yes, sir, and that's about all they have. So we need to keep things in perspective. Not let them push us around."

"And their oil and gas. Putin told me they are the largest producer of oil and gas in the world."

"Oil, yes, gas, no. We are the largest producer of natural gas, and soon may overtake them in oil. And energy is all they have — accounts for 70 percent of their economy. And with oil prices so stagnant, sanctions do hurt."

"Hmm," says POTUS.

"Sir, do you realize that California's economy is larger than Russia's? It's the world's sixth largest, and ..."

"You mean Jerry Brown has a bigger economy than Vladimir Putin?"

"You can look at it that way, sir. The gross national product of the state of California is larger than France's, larger than Italy's, larger than India's. And at $2.6 trillion, it's double the size of Russia's. Russia ranks 13th."

"Wow, I didn't know that," says POTUS. "Democrats — sad, very sad."

"And what's more, when the Brits quit the EU, California will become the fifth largest economy, after the U.S., China, Japan and Germany."

"All that wine and cheese and liberals. And Silicon Valley. At least Peter Thiel likes me."

"Peter Thiel may have founded Pay Pal, but that's not going to win you California."

"Ah, but my commission will find all those ghosts and illegals, the 5 million who voted for Hillary. We'll find them. What else?" says POTUS.

"Sir, I need to be candid. There's a lot of people out there, and a lot in Congress, who want to know why you love Putin so much. Is it true his pals, the oligarchs, helped bail out you and Donald Jr. in 2007 - 2008 with a lot of mon..."

"Very sad, sad, my friend. You're fired."

Trump Either Cannot See the Differences in Values Between the U.S. and Russia or He Doesn't Care
— The Dallas Morning News; September 13, 2017

Donald Trump, meet Bill Browder.

It is unlikely but possible that the president does not know about the history of this American businessman who invested in Russia after the collapse of the Soviet Union, succeeded amazingly but then ran afoul of the Stalinesque barbarity of the current Russian autocracy.

If Trump does know about Browder and his experience in Russia, Trump's bizarre admiration for Vladimir Putin is all the more farcical — especially given the undoubted intervention of Putin's government in the 2016 election.

But let's accept that Trump may have only limited knowledge of what happened to Browder, Hermitage

Capital Management (his investment firm) and his Moscow lawyer, the late, murdered Sergei Magnitsky.

If that's the case, the president needs to read Browder's riveting account of his dealings with Putin's Russia: *Red Notice: A True Story of High Finance, Murder and One Man's Fight for Justice.*

Then Trump should begin to understand the stark difference between American values and Russian preference for order, America's respect for the rule of law and Russia' centuries-long addiction to authoritarianism, America's time-honored freedom of the press and Russia's repression of free speech.

As detailed grippingly in *Red Notice,* Browder's mild-mannered and courageous Russian lawyer Magnitsky was arrested, framed, tortured and killed by Russian authorities in 2008-09 after he refused to collaborate in a high-level conspiracy to cover up the fraudulent seizure of nearly $300 million by Russian investigators from Russia's own treasury.

The case led to congressional passage of the Magnitsky Act in 2012 by overwhelming margins. Co-sponsored by Sens. Ben Cardin, D-Md., and John McCain, R-Ariz., the law barred travel to the U.S. and seized the assets of 60 Russian officials who were involved in Magnitsky's treatment.

Trump should be aware of this case. After passage of the Magnitsky Act, Putin ordered an end to American adoptions of Russian children in retaliation. And it was under the pretext of discussing this issue that Trump's son, Donald Trump Jr., agreed to meet with senior Russian officials during the 2016 campaign — though the real reason was those Russians' offer of "dirt" on Hillary Clinton.

Magnitsky's case is just one of many murders and arbitrary jailings of prominent anti-Putin political figures, wealthy businessmen and leading journalists who wrote about repression and misrule in the last 10 years.

Once the president digests Browder's book, he should begin to realize why a growing number of Americans, even some of his so-called base, are increasingly puzzled and appalled that he cannot bring himself to recognize Russia as a serious threat to the U.S., to international peace and stability.

Yes. Russia possesses a vast arsenal of nuclear weapons — and he needs to start challenging its leaders' violations of critical nuclear accords. He also needs to know that Russia is not the all-powerful country he seems to perceive.

For example, Russia's economy, its total gross domestic product, is one-half the size of the state of California's. California's economy is the sixth-largest in the world; Russia's economy is 13th.

Trump also should realize his affection for Putin only increases suspicions about Russian intervention in the 2016 campaign and Russian investments in Trump properties. His embrace of Putin suggests one of two things: He either admires Putin's near-dictatorial control or he is deathly afraid of him. To paraphrase Shakespeare, "Methinks he protests too much."

Speculation runs wild, of course, and one knows little about what special counsel Robert Mueller and his team are learning as they investigate possible collusion between Russian officials and the Trump campaign.

It is premature to draw conclusions.

John le Carre, one of the most successful novelists in history, and one with a thorough understanding of the internal workings of the Soviet/Russian system, recently made this observation:

"The mentality that is operating in Russia now is absolutely, as far as Putin is concerned, no different to the mentality that drove the most exotic conspiracies during the Cold War. It worked then, and it works now. I suspect they have [embarrassing intelligence on Trump] because they've denied it. If they have it, and they've set Trump up, they'd say, 'Oh, no, we haven't got anything.' But to Trump, they're saying, 'Aren't we being kind to you?'"

Truth or fiction, Mr. President? That's for Trump to come clean about. These matters, as Browder's history and Magnitsky's tragic death make plain, are not "fake news."

Four Facts that Prove Trump is the Most Anti-American President Ever
– *The Dallas Morning News*; December 8, 2017

Donald J. Trump is the most anti-American president in United States history.

Make America Great Again? Hogwash. Trump is on course for making America weak, small, disrespected and dangerous.

Every day, whether it is reckless steps in foreign affairs, yapping about nuclear war, praising the violent acts of white supremacists and recent insults about hardworking professionals of the FBI and our intelligence agencies, Trump makes a fool of himself and the country.

And it's not even clear now that he won the election fairly without immense help from Russia, a proven enemy of the United States and democratic societies everywhere.

Trump does not dare to disprove that millions of dollars were expended by the Russian government, through Facebook and Twitter, through hacks of computers throughout the United States, and through false information distributed by his allies, Wikileaks, to disrupt the election and help his campaign. All he does is repeat a lie: "It's fake news."

The proof of his anti-Americanism lies right before our eyes in his constant abuse of the Constitution, his regular insults against hardworking professionals in the various agencies of the U.S. government and his apparent loyalty to a country, Russia, that is widely considered the most serious threat to American interests and international stability.

Fact: Trump takes a trip abroad, and the most frequent headline is the American president's unceasing criticism of his own country and his predecessors for trade deals or security arrangements, for being mean to his authoritarian friends in Russia and the Philippines.

Fact: Trump's constant assault on thorough newspaper reporting on the corruption, malfeasance and nepotism of his administration is an attack on the First Amendment. His constant description of first-rate newspapers as "the enemy of the people" is repeating a favorite phrase of the former Soviet Union and Russia.

Fact: All American intelligence agencies have agreed that the Russian government intervened in the 2016 presidential election. There is no dispute, except in Donald Trump's head, that such interference took place. Yet, Trump has called intelligence agents "Nazis." And this White House wants its own cadre of spies? The very tactic a dictatorship might try.

Fact: On foreign policy, we have a president who is withdrawing the United States from critical international institutions that were largely created and led by the U.S. for decades. By reducing America's role in the United Nations, withdrawing from the Trans-Pacific Trade Partnership, yielding economic leadership in Asia to China and pulling out of the climate-change accord because it's a "Chinese hoax," Trump pushes the U.S. into a rudderless, isolationist position. The move to place our embassy in Jerusalem not only wipes out the historic role of the U.S. as an honest broker in the Middle East, but it also endangers Americans.

And the move by Trump and his Secretary of State to downgrade and dismantle the State Department underline this president's lack of judgment and leadership in complex international affairs. Experienced diplomatic engagement is always critical, all the more so with Trump's reckless threats of military force all across the globe.

And then there's Trump's bizarre affection for Russia and Vladimir Putin. The investigation by special counsel Robert Mueller is unfolding, but it has already unmasked several top Trump aides for supporting Russian interests: Gen. Michael "Lock Her Up" Flynn and Trump campaign chairman Paul Manafort. No wonder 50 leading GOP national security experts condemned Trump in 2016.

With his embrace of a totalitarian regime that has invaded Crimea and Ukraine and poses a threat to democratic countries, with Flynn and other aides' efforts to help Russia resist U.S. sanctions, there appear to be only three conclusions to explain Trump's embrace of Russia:

1. He is truly clueless: TV reality stars tend to tune out reality.

2. He knows that Putin and Co. have something on him, *compromat* in Russian (or dirt) — the kind Donald Trump Jr.

sought on Hillary Clinton from secret meetings with Russian agents.

3. His highly leveraged real estate empire was or is heavily in debt to Russian investors — a fact Donald Jr. admitted was true after the 2007-08 financial crisis.

Nearly a year ago, Trump put his hand on a Bible and swore to "preserve, protect and defend the Constitution of the United States." With a spate of lies, insults and reckless decisions across the board, lacking any moral compass himself on the treatment of women, isolating the United States from its closest friends and allies, Donald J. Trump has spent most of the year trampling on that sacred oath and is a disgrace to this great nation and its people.

Give the White, Blue, and Red for Christmas – *Bangor Daily News*; December 23, 2018

A perfect gift this year for most Republican senators and representatives is the good old white, blue and red.

That's right; you read it correctly. Not the red, white and blue flag of the United States of America, but the tricolor of the Russian Federation.

The meek — almost silent — reaction of the Republican Party to Russian interference in the 2016 election, now documented as having blanketed the U.S., has been so craven and cowardly, there is only one way to reward them:

Send them the Russian flag to wave in their congressional offices.

Most GOP members of Congress today, their Fox News propagandists and many on the right are supporting Russia by turning their backs on the facts: hard evidence that the Russian government has waged a widespread attack on the United States with everything from a blitzkrieg wave of vicious lies and false information on social media to millions of dollars of financial support for the National Rifle Association, a major Trump backer.

Dozens of respected conservative columnists and national security leaders have recognized and condemned Russia's interference — and denounced Trump and the GOP: George Will, Eliot Cohen, Michael Hayden, Max Boot, Bret Stephens. But only a handful of GOP members of Congress have done so, and several are leaving office. The late Sen. John McCain boldly condemned the Russian campaign, describing Russian leader Vladimir Putin as a murderer and thug.

As a result of the relative silence from other Republicans, Trump has been emboldened to continue to call the investigation into Russian interference a "witch-hunt."

Congressional Republicans have largely shied away from bipartisan efforts to protect the Mueller probe despite daily evidence of Russia's attack: A new Senate report on a wholesale attack by Russia's Internet Research Agency to engage Americans on social media; 25 Russian nationals being indicted by the special counsel for alleged identity theft and hacking of Democratic Party communications;

several high-level Trump figures, including his first national security adviser, Michael Flynn, pleading guilty to conspiring with Russian officials; a young Russian gun-rights advocate agreed to plead guilty to acting as a foreign agent; millions of dollars invested in Trump properties by Russian oligarchs; and Trump's obsequious approach to Russia and personal meetings with Putin, going so far at a Helsinki meeting to accept Putin's denial of Russian interference over the unanimous conclusion of American intelligence agencies.

The campaign to interfere in US elections dates back many years, but it gained steam during the Obama administration, when Putin shifted course from a post-1991 policy to engage with the West to instead sow division within the Western alliance.

Putin has done so with both aggressive and sophisticated measures, ranging from outright invasion of an independent Ukraine to massive cyberattacks on Western democracies.

Russia's strategy, basically to weaken the United States by exploiting internal tensions, reverses the old Soviet-era strategy to seek support within America through the left wing, partly through unions that tended to support socialist policies. For the past decade, the Russian government has focused all its efforts on the right wing — once the most virulently anti-Russian of Americans.

Tom Nichols, an analyst at the Naval War College, recently noted the ironic, 180-degree shift in Moscow's tactics. In the old days, the Soviets saw their opening on the left; now

Russia seeks to slice into the American polity on the right, and many in the GOP are playing right into their hands with their fear of Trump.

Nichols, a lifelong conservative until Trump, has warned of "an accelerating hostility towards established knowledge" in the ideological shift in the GOP and their acceptance of Trump's disdain for expertise and the rule of law.

Republicans afraid to criticize Trump's refusal to recognize Russia's assault need to read one of Alexander Hamilton's essays in the 1787 Federalist Papers.

"One of the weak sides of republics, among their numerous advantages, is that they afford too easy an inlet to foreign corruption," Hamilton wrote in Federalist No. 22, later discussing the possibility for "a foreign power with which we were at war to perplex our councils and embarrass our exertions."

Maine Voices: Faithful Defense of Russia, Putin Reflects Poorly on Today's Republicans
– The Portland Press Herald; December 10, 2019

Two of the most infamous Joes in history – McCarthy and Stalin – would be stunned by the Republican Party's embrace of Russia these days, its leader, Vladimir Putin, and a Russia-loving American president, Donald J. Trump.

Joseph McCarthy, the fear-mongering, anti-communist senator, and Josef Stalin, the dictator of the former Soviet Union who oversaw the murder of millions of his own citizens, then including Ukrainians, would be astonished by the actions and words of Republicans from Trump to Republican members of Congress such as Devin Nunes of California, Jim Jordan of Ohio and John Ratcliffe of Texas.

The impeachment hearings are focused on Trump's pressure campaign to withhold critical military aid to Ukraine, essential to defend itself against Russian aggression, in return for political favors.

Testimony to date makes it clear that President Trump and his personal attorney, Rudy Giuliani, blocked $391 million in weapons to Ukraine and a White House meeting unless its new leadership undertook an investigation of the Biden family's involvement with a Ukrainian energy company.

The proceedings are not going well for the president and his defenders. Witnesses have testified that Trump and Giuliani withheld that assistance unless it received a promise to help Trump with his political challenges.

Defying White House orders not to testify, Ambassador Gordon Sondland, a $1 million donor to Trump, confirmed that the Trump-Giuliani pressure was a "quid pro quo."

A career ambassador, William Taylor, testified that he objected to Trump pressure to block the aid – critical to Ukraine's ability to fight Russia's aggression. Fiona Hill, a leading expert, said: "Please don't promote politically driven falsehoods that so clearly advance Russian interests."

Hill put her finger on the larger context of the matter: that President Trump and the Republican Party have become faithful and frequent defenders of Russia and Putin.

A few facts:

• Russia committed the only major aggression against a sovereign nation in Europe since World War II.

Russia seized Crimea and invaded eastern Ukraine after a popular revolution in 2014 that chased away a pro-Moscow leader, Viktor Yanukovych, and led to a pro-Western government. Over 13,000 Ukrainians have died in the last five years of Russian occupation of eastern Ukraine.

• The pro-Moscow Yanukovych is believed to have absconded with over $30 billion when he fled to Moscow. Trump's campaign chairman, Paul Manafort, who advised Yanukovych, is now in prison for seven years on corruption charges.

• Donald Trump has leaned over backward, beginning before his 2016 election, to befriend and be helpful to Russia and Putin.

Trump regularly praises Putin. His aides watered down the Republican convention platform on U.S. support for Ukraine's democracy. He has frequently opposed bipartisan sanctions on Russia's struggling economy – which is one half that of California's.

• Republican members of Congress continually ignore the conclusion of all American intelligence agencies, the Mueller probe and the Republican-led Senate Intelligence Committee that there was "massive" Russian interference in the campaign in favor of Trump.

• In addition to Russia's cyberwar for Trump, millions were invested in Trump properties by Russian oligarchs over the years. Russian gun rights groups reportedly gave $30 million to the National Rifle Association. The NRA spent the same on Trump.

• The National Security Strategy of the U.S. government formally cites Russia as a major threat to the United States, saying it seeks to "erode" American power and values.

In a continuing attack on America's historical alliances and allies, Trump said Russia should return to the G-7; it was ejected after invading Ukraine.

After the 2018 Helsinki summit, Trump said he trusted the word of Putin that Russia did not intervene in the 2016 U.S. election, dismissing all American intelligence.

Lastly, whenever he is criticized by American newspapers, Trump derides them as "the enemy of the people," a term popularized by Josef Stalin.

If he were here today, and restaging his scurrilous hearings on "un-American activities," Joe McCarthy, eventually disgraced and chased from office, in part because of the courageous voice of Maine Sen. Margaret Chase Smith, the Wisconsin senator would look up and see that his only defendants and witnesses were today's Republicans – now routinely placing Russian interests ahead of the U.S. Constitution, the rule of law and our democratic values.

Part IV. Make America Alone Again

From his cavalier abuse of America's closest allies and alliances that won the Cold War such as NATO to his withdrawal from any serious international agreement made by his predecessor, Barack Obama, such as the Iran nuclear accord and the Paris Climate Accord, Donald John Trump has gravely diminished the reputation of the United States as a global leader.

After three and a half years of Trump's presidency, the United States is no longer respected as the world's leader and most stable, successful democracy. The nation's word is no better than a "tweet-storm" by Trump away. The United States is no longer seen as a stable, pragmatic super-power – but an unpredictable, unreliable and selfish nation. No respectable leader on earth can trust a country whose president is a serial liar.

With a revolving door of advisers he fired as soon as many of them stood up to him and told him he was wrong, Donald Trump has overseen a precipitous decline in respect for the United States on the world stage.

Leaders of the world have even taken to ignoring him or, behind his back as at a G-20 meeting in 2018, making fun of him. Trump's motto, MAGA, is now nothing more than MAAA – Make America Alone Again.

He has succeeded at virtually nothing in three plus years in office. His ill-advised embrace of North Korea's dictator Kim Jung Un has resulted in Kim's playing him like a fool –

insulting Trump as a "dotard," continuing to fire off missiles, and blowing up the building where they first met.

Trump's withdrawal from the Iran nuclear accord agreed by President Obama with all major world powers, has yielded no new improvement in Iranian behavior and led to an escalation in tensions and the danger of war. Iran is closer to a nuclear weapon thanks to Trump.

His contempt for science – and Barack Obama – led him to deride climate change as "a Chinese hoax"- against the near-unanimous consensus of the world's scientists, and set the stage for the horrific ignorant response to the 2020 pandemic. Trump has even disdained nuclear weapons treaties. While Russian pursuit of new weapons, and desire to compensate for its weak economic throw-weight is partly to blame, the Trump administration has shown little interest in renewing critical nuclear treaties, the supreme and bipartisan achievements of Republican and Democratic administrations. Even a loyal Republican such as former Reagan Secretary of State George Shultz has said the Trump administration is at fault for the so-called Doomsday clock being closer to midnight than at the height of the Cold War.

(Note # 3).

Even on issues that deserved a tough policy, Trump's approach lacked broad strategic approach and finesse. He instigated a trade war with China – not necessarily a bad idea given China's opposition to U.S. imports and theft of intellectual property. Yet, Trump bulldozed on alone, when he might have joined forces with European powers and accomplished much more. According to his third national security adviser, John Bolton, Trump begged Chinese leaders for concessions to help him get reelected – and backed Chinese concentration camps for ethnic dissidents.

On trade, he tore up the Trans-Pacific Partnership – an action that benefitted only China. He tore up the NAFTA agreement with Canada and Mexico, replacing it with a remarkably similar arrangements.

And on a campaign promise to end American wars, the Trump administration pursued an erratic policy in the Middle East. He frequently claimed to have defeated ISIS; far from the truth. He named an utterly clue-less son-in-law to head his "Middle East Peace Plan." His efforts to withdraw U.S. troops from Afghanistan have led to sporadic yet far from positive results.

The bankruptcy of Trump's foreign policy is reflected in the revolving door of senior advisers in the key national security agencies – Defense, State, the National Security Council, the intelligence community. In his fourth year, Donald Trump is now being served by a mix of third and fourth-rate advisers – whose main qualification is loyalty to Trump.

Michael Pompeo, his Secretary of State, is a Christian evangelical who once said he thought Trump was placed on earth to save Israel. Pompeo has shown cowardice and complicity in Trumplandia by repeatedly failing to stand up for the diplomatic corps, standing meekly aside as Trump smeared the "deep State department." He has pursued regime change, risking a possible war, with Iran.

Pompeo and other Trump stalwarts listened in on the president's phone calls to pressure Ukraine into investigating his likely rival Joe Biden. But they made no effort to stop what was clearly misguided, impeachable behavior.

Trump's "America First" doctrine led to even worse embarrassment during the cataclysmic Covid-19 pandemic when he not only denied its severity and offered erratic leadership in the United States, but blocked multi-lateral assistance to poorer countries and withdrew the United States from the World Health Organization.

Life-long Republicans do not give him credit for much of any achievement in foreign policy. Richard Haass, now head of the Council of Foreign Relations, labelled Trump's policies "The Withdrawal Doctrine."

Lawrence Wilkerson, chief of staff to Colin Powell, then Secretary of State in the George W. Bush administration, sums it up starkly: "In terms of the damage done to America – international and domestic, substantive and reputational, fiscal and economic – Trump has no peer on record. Electing a new president in November will help stop the ravages, but Trump has been so utterly disastrous it will take a generation to recover."

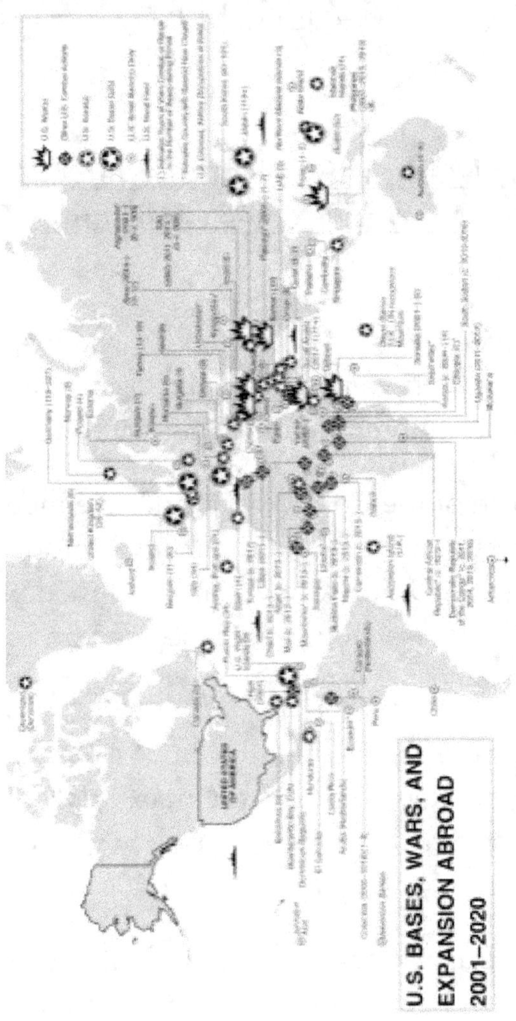

The number and far-flung presence of U.S. military bases reflects the global extent of American interests and commitments.

Credit: Kelly Martin Design/David Vine in David Vine, The United States of War: A Global History of America's Endless Conflicts, from Columbus to the Islamic State (University of California Press, October, 2020).

118

Trump Has Made U.S. a Rogue State – *The Dallas Morning News* with James Goodby; June 13, 2017

The U.S. has been blessed with leaders who inspired us and the world with their vision, their purpose, their sense of history and commitment to international rules.

In the cauldron of the Cold War, John F. Kennedy stood in Berlin and declared "I am a Berliner" in a compelling speech that let the Soviet Union know that the United States and the Western democracies would not be cowed by Soviet threats and tanks.

Ronald Reagan spoke eloquently about America as a shining city on a hill, challenging us to set an example for democracies and dictatorships, daring Soviet leaders to "tear down" the Berlin Wall.

George H.W. Bush oversaw the potentially explosive collapse of the Soviet Union and its empire with restraint, and shrewdly negotiated German reunification. Franklin Roosevelt reminded the country in the midst of the Great Depression that "the only thing we have to fear is fear itself." Despite facing partisan gridlock, President Barack Obama regularly appealed to our better nature.

With exceptions, we have been fortunate to have leaders who inspired us to new heights and led a partnership of nations in a troubled world. They spoke of American exceptionalism, of America as the "indispensable nation." American presidents generally observed the Declaration of Independence plea to "respect the opinions of mankind."

Today, we have in Donald J. Trump a rude, reckless and thin-skinned president who, with both tweet-driven comments and decisions, is doing his best to turn this great country into what former Irish president Mary Robinson views as " a rogue state."

A few examples of Trump's erratic behavior suggest the U.S., under a Trumpian administration, no longer intends to remain within the network of rules and norms that define relationships among the democracies of the world.

- Rejection of the Paris climate accord, a voluntary agreement that joined the U.S. with virtually all nations to tackle global warming, a widely recognized phenomenon Trump calls a "Chinese hoax."
- Abuse of European allies and the NATO alliance, which has helped secure peace for 70 years. Trump ignored the advice of key foreign policy advisers to express American commitment to Article 5 of the NATO treaty, which pledges support for all members if one is attacked. The only time the article has been invoked was after 9/11 when all other members stood by the United States.

- While insulting German leaders whose companies produce thousands of jobs in the southern U.S., Trump embraces authoritarian leaders in countries like Russia and the Philippines. He repeatedly expresses admiration for Russia's Vladimir Putin, the invader of Crimea and Ukraine, whose country sent hackers to disrupt the last presidential election.
- Trump has shown little interest in the critical issue of nuclear proliferation. If anything, he has talked about acquiring more weapons, ignored Russian violations of existing treaties and been willing to subcontract nuclear diplomacy in Asia to a reluctant China.

Herewith a few modest suggestions to restore confidence in the U.S. commitment to international leadership and democratic values.

1. Trump appointed competent individuals to lead his national security team. Yet, time and again, as in the Article 5 commitment, he repeatedly ignores their advice.

2. Stop the tweeting. Trump's impulsive, humorless reactions embarrass him and the country, as in his charge that Obama tapped his phones and his criticism of the mayor of London (a Muslim) after the latest terrorist attack. The presidency is not a TV-reality show.

3. Open the books, disclose all contacts with Russia. Release tax returns. The investigation(s) will continue.

4. Revise the message conveyed by a recent *Wall Street Journal* article by Gary Cohn and Gen. H.R. McMaster on

the intent of the president's strategy. To say nations have only interests and national motives may explain why Trump admires Putin and withdraws from the Paris accord, but it rejects the vision and shared values that have been the centerpiece of the Western alliance since World War II.

What are the characteristics of a rogue state? It is a nation that refuses to join other nations as stewards of the planet, as the United Nations Charter set out; a nation that favors disruption and threats of violence over diplomacy as the primary way to solve complex challenges; and a nation for which every relationship is based on win or lose, profit or loss.

In an increasingly globalizing world, where nuclear proliferation, terrorism and environmental disaster demand truly international cooperation, such narrow, selfish mind-sets speak of a fascistlike, me-first mentality and gravely weaken efforts to address them effectively.

It's Time to Formally End the Koren War Before Tensions Trigger a New One
– *The Dallas Morning News* with James Goodby; July 13, 2017

We must not stumble into another war on the Korean peninsula, one that could lead to the use of nuclear weapons and the deaths of millions, before we have tried far more vigorously to bring an end to the first Korean War.

The most dangerous and explosive problem in the world today stems in part from a failure to formally end that brutal war. The Korean War is, in effect, still going on — 64 years later.

Hostilities that unfolded after the June 1950 North Korean invasion of South Korea were only suspended by the armistice signed on July 27, 1953. President Dwight Eisenhower praised the courage and steadfastness of the 16 nations that thwarted the North Korean attack with "decisive purpose." After the longest negotiated armistice talks in history, he declared: "And so at long last, the carnage of war is to cease and the negotiation of the conference table is to begin."

Only the negotiation never really began. The armistice is not a peace treaty between nations; it is simply a military document. Today, it is effectively moribund, except for the Demilitarized Zone of 4,000 meters that separates the forces of the two countries and, in the south, 23,500 members of the U. S. military.

After more than a decade of various strategies, from dark threats to engagement to "strategic patience," it is clear that the major powers involved, especially the U.S. and China, are running out of good options to dissuade North Korea from a precipitous threat to wreak havoc in Asia and the world with its headlong pursuit of both an intercontinental ballistic missile and a miniaturized nuclear device that could reach the U.S.

A return to the negotiating table, therefore, is the inevitable next step. Despite the failures of past talks, there is no other recourse.

Given the geography of the Korean peninsula and the deployment of North Korea's army and artillery 35 miles north of South Korea's capital, Seoul, even a massive pre-emptive strike would lead to the death of millions of people.

A freeze on tests of North Korea's missiles and nuclear weapons would be highly desirable, but bitter experience has shown that a broader basis for cooperation is essential to keep the process going. One major step that could place all parties on the path to resolution of fundamental differences in the U.S. relationship with North Korea, not to mention a relaxation of tensions for the entire region, would be to discuss a peace treaty to end the Korean War.

There are several sound reasons to take this approach.

- It is long overdue.
- Problematic as it may be, it may well appeal to the young and temperamental North Korean leader, Kim Jong Un, and set the stage for broader, more conclusive negotiations.
- And it may encourage China to take a more forceful role in negotiations than it has shown since President Donald Trump's Mar-a-Lago meeting with Chinese President Xi Jinping and repeated efforts to get

China, North Korea's sole benefactor, to pressure the hermit kingdom into more responsible behavior.

Beijing is hesitant to pressure the North on the nuclear issue for fear of a collapse of the current dictatorship in Pyongyang and a migration of millions into China.

Trump should abandon his strong-arm demands of President Xi. Instead, he should ask for help opening a dialogue with Kim Jong Un, to prevent another Otto Warmbeir tragedy and to ensure all Korean people can thrive, without fear of a nuclear catastrophe just around the corner.

Xi might be ready to convene a conference to examine prospects to complete a peace treaty. North Korea is likely to demand a treaty only with the U.S., excluding South Korea. But parties should be able to finesse that impediment after seven decades of confrontation and recognition of the South's dynamic success. The roles of the U.S. and China would be placed in their proper context in such four-party talks — as their roles in the war played out.

Once a peace treaty — final or interim — is in place, further negotiations could lead to talks on measures to build confidence, such as hotlines to prevent accidental clashes, and then to more sensitive questions such as the North's military deployments, U.S.-Korean exercises and a nuclear freeze. In time, both Japan and Russia could be invited to join the talks.

Eventually, one could envision seriously considering lifting sanctions on North Korea in return for de-nuclearization, commitments to withdraw forces from tense borders, expanded economic cooperation, and stability on the peninsula.

Trump's National Security Strategy Makes Sense, and That Has Little to Do with Trump
– *The Dallas Morning News; December 28, 2017*

Shortly after the Trump administration's national security strategy hit the street two weeks ago, one of the president's most significant steps in foreign policy was condemned by virtually every country in the world.

Donald Trump's decision to recognize Jerusalem as the capital of Israel drew the support of a number of powerhouses: Togo, Guatemala and Honduras. Also, Nauru and Palau — tiny island nations in the Pacific Ocean.

Britain, France, Germany, Japan, China, Russia and Saudi Arabia all voted along with most major countries of the United Nations to condemn the decision (128-9, with 35 abstentions) and demand its reversal.

Bad timing? Perhaps. The Trump presidency did have narrow passage of a so-called tax reform to celebrate — even though its main beneficiaries are the wealthiest 1 percent, not the lower and middle classes he promised to help.

It was bad timing in the sense that the new strategy, one required of every administration periodically, actually made some sense. While bearing much continuity with the national security strategy papers of Barack Obama and George W. Bush, the new version reflected some of Trump's campaign rhetoric.

Trump's strategy is a reasonably sound set of principles and lofty goals on many important issues, though it eliminates climate change as a serious national concern.

It fails to offer much strategic vision; it does not spell out concrete objectives or specific steps to achieve them. For instance, the paper runs on about Iran's growing influence, saying little about how to counter it. Yet other administrations have been guilty of similar shortcomings in explaining how they would accomplish their goals.

However, the document's most glaring failure, noted Richard Haass, president of the Council on Foreign Relations, is the complete "disconnect" between its critical goals and Trump's words and actions in the first year of his presidency.

Haass, a national security adviser to several Republican presidents, and other experts underlined many instances of this gap shortly after release of the document.

Example: The NSS contains many references to "American democracy and values." Trump has shown complete disdain for the Constitution in his attacks on the press, highly professional government agents and the American system of justice.

Example: The document says "we must upgrade our diplomatic capabilities," a sound idea when one tweets casually about using military force, even nuclear weapons. Yet Trump and his secretary of state have butchered the State Department and moved to get rid of respected veterans.

Example: The document clearly marks Russia and China as rivals and sharply criticizes these "revisionist powers" for their use of cyberwarfare. Yet Trump has withdrawn from key trade partnerships in the Pacific, emboldening and enhancing China's influence, and has leaned over backward to be nice to Russia and Vladimir Putin. He even continues to deny there was any Russian interference in the 2016 election despite the 100 percent conclusion of all of our intelligence agencies.

Example: One of the most ludicrous assertions is this: The U.S. "will encourage those struggling for human dignity in their societies." That is a stark contradiction of Trump's embrace of autocratic rulers in Russia, the Philippines and Turkey, his attitude toward immigrants fleeing oppression and lack of interest in human rights.

Nicholas Burns, another senior official from GOP administrations, criticized Trump's failure to promote democracy and freedom: "He's weakening us on these essential foundations of American power."

In other words, the new NSS is a worthy statement of American values and interests of the past and future. But it is a very distorted, if not blatantly false, portrayal of the current policies of Trump — at least to date.

This president does have several sensible, experienced leaders who help to offset his own blank slate in foreign affairs and his juvenile, TV-reality-level tweets. Two respected generals, Defense Secretary James Mattis and national security adviser H.R. McMaster, clearly played a major role in production of this document.

Yet, other than presumed restraint on Trump's worst impulses, his advisers have not prevented a grave weakening of American influence in the world in the first year of his presidency. The conservative Economist magazine recently concluded: "For all its flaws, America has long been the greatest force for good in the world. All that is imperiled by a president who believes that strong nations look out only for themselves. By putting 'America First,' Trump makes it weaker, and the world worse off."

The new NSS purports to be based on "principled realism" as its framework. In his first year as president, from crude attacks on reporters, judges and FBI and intelligence agents, moves to withdraw the U.S. from multilateral international institutions, embrace of authoritarian leaders and repeated lies and insults that demean the office of the presidency, Trump has shown little respect for either principle or realism.

Trump Ought to be Careful about Throwing around the T-word
– *The Dallas Morning News*; February 7, 2018

As he approaches another election next month, Russian President Vladimir Putin must be chortling in his afternoon tea or evening vodka.

Putin stands to be elected for the fourth time, with a large majority in a quasi-democratic election -- only partly democratic when a leader arrests his strongest opponent and tightly controls the media.

And Putin benefits from having an American president, many members of the Republican majority in Congress and a major news outlet, Fox News, in his back pocket.

What else can one conclude from the following developments, after heavy-handed Russian intervention in the 2016 election:

- President Donald Trump just blocked imposition of stiff sanctions against Russia that were approved by a vast majority of Congress. Little reaction from Congress or Fox commentators.
- Trump continues to condemn the investigation of Russian intervention in the election -- not the intervention -- despite confirmation of the full-bore cyber attacks and his own aides pleading guilty to lying about Russian contacts.
- Trump's own son, Donald Trump Jr., held secret meetings with leading Russians during the campaign

to gain Russian dirt on Hillary Clinton. And he lied about it.

- Trump repeatedly impugns the patriotism and integrity of major institutions in the U.S. government, particularly the FBI and the CIA (whose agents he has called "Nazis,") and regularly shows disdain for the U.S. Constitution and key protections of a free press and freedom of religion.

- After release of a classified memo that questioned an FBI probe of a Trump aide with close brushes with Russian spies, a release that Trump eagerly backed, Sen. John McCain, R-Ariz., said: "The Russian government engaged in an elaborate plot to interfere in our election and undermine American democracy." Noting Trump's criticism of the FBI, McCain added: "If we continue to undermine our own rule of law, we are doing Putin's work for him."

- Trump's business empire, once wobbly from multiple bankruptcies and the 2007-2008 meltdown, drew heavily on investments and purchases by wealthy Russian oligarchs, many close friends of Putin's.

- Trump, as candidate and president, has repeatedly embraced the Russian leader despite his own security strategy's description of Russia as a major threat to American interests. Under Putin, Russia committed the only major aggression in Europe since World War II in its seizure of Crimea and intervention in Ukraine.

Perhaps just as bizarre as Trump's cozy attitude toward Russia are the actions of many Republicans in Congress and on Fox News. Here are people who in past decades turned purple and vociferous in their attacks on basically the same country. Today, many GOP members and Fox News commentators are quick to defend Trump and his stance toward Russia even though Russia retains many attributes of the Communist empire.

The special counsel's investigation of Russian interference in the 2016 presidential election will come to its climactic finish in time. Collusion? Obstruction of justice? Impeachment? No charges? It is too early to predict.

But a more serious charge against the 45th president could be looming if he continues to speak and act as if Russia were America's best ally.

Article III, Section 3 of the Constitution states: "Treason against the United States shall consist only in levying war against them [the states plural], or, in adhering to their enemies, giving them aid and comfort."

Unlike the Soviet Union, Russia is no longer considered an "enemy" of the United States. It is, according to the recent defense strategy a "revisionist" power that poses a major threat to "the security and prosperity of the U.S." But one more aggressive act could revert us back to Cold War relations.

And guess who just threw around the charge of treason as if it were an everyday allegation? Trump. And he set a low bar. In an appearance Monday, he said Democrats may have acted "treasonously" when they did not applaud his much-faulted tax reform package during the State of the Union address.

However, it is Trump who is enmeshed in an investigation into whether a foreign nation meddled in the presidential election to his benefit. Damning evidence against Trump and his friendly behavior toward Russia emerged last week. On the program Fresh Air, a respected Israeli journalist, Ronen Bergman, said that the highly classified information that Trump disclosed to Russian Foreign Minister Sergei Lavrov last May in the White House was extremely secret.

Bergman said that senior Israeli intelligence agents were warned in late 2016 by American counterparts that "Trump or some of his people [may be] under leverage from the Russians." Then, Bergman added, "just a few months after that ... all the predictions came to be true. I know the nature of that information. It is indeed delicate, and very, very secret. It could jeopardize the modus operandi of Israeli intelligence." (See note 2).

A president has broad authority to declassify government secrets. Yet that authority has little to do with whether he acted recklessly and gave "aid and comfort" to a dangerous adversary. Be careful, Mr. President, we don't know where the Russia investigation will yet end up.

<u>With Trump's Withdrawal from Iran Nuclear Deal, the Chicken Hawks are Back</u>
<u>– *The Dallas Morning News; May 9, 2018*</u>

The chicken hawks are back.

If you liked the invasion of Iraq by the Bush-Cheney administration, the catastrophic war that badly stained international respect for the U.S., damaged its economy and set the stage for the rise of ISIS, then you'll love what may be in the wings as President Donald Trump withdrew from the Iran nuclear agreement, an accord won through tough diplomacy by the Obama administration and supported by all major powers.

Trump's decision ignores the advice of his ablest strategic counselor, Secretary of Defense James Mattis, European leaders and most experts in the U.S. who argue the accord prevents the very threat Trump considers so serious.

Trump's unilateral act embraces the arguments of many of the neo-conservatives who pushed the U.S. into war with Iraq on equally spurious grounds, and thumbs his nose at leaders of all of the leading countries in the world, who see the accord as the best means to block Iran from the pursuit of nuclear weapons. It also suggests to North Korea's leaders on the eve of critical negotiations that the U.S. does not keep its word.

And withdrawal comes without any serious strategy to deal with Iran except a potential confrontation, as Iran is likely to renew its uranium enrichment now, heightening the possibility of war in the Middle East.

Sadly, as 50 leading Republican national security experts warned during the 2016 campaign, we have an inexperienced, reckless leader in the White House, one who does not even understand key details of the accord. For example, Trump says that under the accord Iran can begin producing nuclear weapons in seven years. Wrong. The 2015 agreement severely restricts production of enriched uranium until 2030, provides strict international inspections and restores all sanctions in the event of violations.

Other than Mattis and Secretary of State Mike Pompeo, two of the four most important decision-makers on the Iran accord are what we can call chicken hawks: Trump and his new national security adviser John Bolton.

There is no known species of the *Accipiter* (hawk) genus called chicken hawks. The term was popular during the Vietnam War when people were often divided into pro-war "hawks" and anti-war "doves." The colloquial meaning of "chicken" is well-known -- fearful, timid.

In the run-up to the invasion of Iraq in 2003, a majority of the leading decision-makers in the Bush-Cheney White House who favored war were chicken hawks -- men (no women) in favor of war who had dodged the draft or avoided front-line military service. Example No. 1: Vice President Richard Cheney gained five deferments so he would not have to serve in the military.

President George W. Bush served in the Texas Air National Guard. Otherwise, only Defense Secretary Donald Rumsfeld and Secretary of State Colin Powell served in the military and thereby knew the agony and unexpected consequences of combat. The balance of key officials who took the country headlong into a disastrous war were people who dodged the draft or had ducked any conflict: Cheney, Paul Wolfowitz, Douglas Feith and, among others, Bolton.

Bolton famously wrote in his Yale alumni yearbook: "I confess I had no desire to die in a Southeast Asia rice paddy."

Trump and Bolton have a lot in common. They both went to military schools in their youth. Yet both declined to serve in the real military. Trump turned out to have "bone spurs" in 1968 and gained five draft deferments. Bolton joined the National Guard to avoid being sent to Vietnam.

A better strategy to tackle Iran is focusing on a broader, more comprehensive set of issues. While maintaining a rigorous policy against reckless Iranian military ventures, the Trump administration could focus on human rights and the lack of freedom of information in Iran, for instance. Iran does have an aggressive foreign policy, one encouraged by the U.S. disaster in Iraq. And there is good reason to take steps to counter Iran's growing influence, support for terrorism and antagonism for Israel.

Trump should go to the United Nations and demand the freedom of innocent Iranian-Americans like Baquer and Siamak Namazi, father and son jailed by the regime for no reason. Or a Princeton doctoral student, Xiyue Wang, who went to study ancient history but was arrested and sentenced to 10 years in prison. Or condemn the recent execution of a leading Iranian environmentalist.

The president could highlight the Iranian government's constant clamp-down on freedom of speech, seen in many other jailings or its recent ban on Telegram, the main social media platform for 40 million Iranians.

Trump does not seem interested in pursuing those avenues of challenge to Iran's bad behavior because he shows no interest in human rights or freedom of information. In these cases, he basically aligns with Iran's ayatollahs: It's all "fake news."

Trump Team Threatens National Security – *The Baltimore Sun*; January 15, 2019

If you're worried about the security of the United States after President Donald Trump's disgraceful dismissal of Gen. James Mattis as Secretary of Defense, you also need to look inside the U.S. government to examine the Trump hangers-on who are downgrading the professionalism of key government agencies.

For example, on Inauguration Day, according to Michael Lewis in his new book, "The Fifth Risk," Mr. Trump, utterly unprepared for governing after a narrow victory, sent these folks to help run the Department of Agriculture: "A long-haul truck driver, a telephone company clerk, a gas company meter reader, a country club cabana attendant, a Republican National Committee intern and the owner of a scented candle company."

Similar appointments of political faithful and lobbyists with scant knowledge or strong industry positions were made throughout the U.S. government, including in agencies responsible for nuclear waste, food safety and hurricane warnings. A 23-year-old Trump campaign worker was named deputy head of the opioid crisis office in the White House. These Trump lieutenants ordered data suppression throughout multiple agencies.

The dumbing down of the American government, a condition that starts at the top with a president who brags that he does not read books or need intelligence briefings, extends to Capitol Hill.

As the 116th Congress opens, look no further than the two most important committees on national security in the U. S. Senate.

Gone is the late John McCain, who chaired the Armed Services Committee for years with knowledge, deep experience in military matters and courage — and a readiness to stand up to Mr. Trump's fanboy relationship with Russian president Vladimir Putin.

Also gone are smart, bipartisan ex-chairmen such as Republican John Warner and Democrats Carl Levin and Sam Nunn. Mr. Nunn worked with Republicans after the collapse of the Soviet Union to craft vital legislation on dismantling its nuclear, biological and chemical weapons.

Now the chairman is 84-year-old James H. Inhofe of Oklahoma. Senator Inhofe's own official biography says "our country is in the most threatened position in American history…" Really, Senator?

Has Mr. Inhofe forgotten the Cold War and the daily threat of nuclear annihilation from the Soviet Union? The gravity of the Cuban missile crisis? World War II, Pearl Harbor, the Depression, the 2008 financial meltdown?

Mr. Inhofe, who has called climate change "the greatest hoax," is responsible for foisting on the government the services of Scott Pruitt, the disgraced former head of the Environmental Protection Agency and several former Inhofe aides, who have been able to trash dozens of environmental protections, including an order to roll back rules designed to protect 60 percent of the nation's water bodies.

Like Mr. Pruitt, Mr. Inhofe has been accused of corrupt practices — buying large amounts of the stock of a giant defense contractor after urging Mr. Trump to increase the defense budget significantly. He sold the stock.

Another key Senate committee — the Senate Foreign Relations Committee — is being turned over to an equally unremarkable senator: Idaho Sen. James Risch, 75, a former governor who gained that position by appointment.

Another climate change denier and an A+ NRA supporter who "prayed" for the victims of the various shooting massacres but opposes background checks, Mr. Risch is an unabashed supporter of Mr. Trump.

Compare his credentials to his predecessors. Sen. Richard Lugar, Republican of Indiana and chairman for two terms, worked tirelessly with Senator Nunn on nuclear dismantlement. Idaho Democrat Frank Church oversaw investigations of intelligence abuses. J. William Fulbright, Democrat of Arkansas, helped manage the Johnson administration's misguided Gulf of Tonkin resolution but redeemed himself with careful, balanced explorations of the causes and mistakes of the Vietnam war. And Arthur Vandenberg, Republican of Michigan, was a moderate of the kind GOP leaders might seek out to regain respect for their party in the age of Mr. Trump.

At the end of World War II, Vandenberg delivered a courageous speech in which he declared that partisan politics "must stop at the water's edge." He went on to cooperate with President Truman in the establishment of the Marshall Plan and the North Atlantic Treaty Organization (NATO) — both linchpins of the Western alliance ever since.

And who is doing his utmost to undermine both organizations today, putting in grave question America's national interests and international leadership?

A Republican president: Donald J. Trump.

Donald Trump's Lack of Credibility Complicates Dangerous Iran Situation
– *Bangor Daily News; August 1, 2019*

"Totally false," Donald Trump tweeted about the Iranian government's claim of arresting 17 people for spying for the Central Intelligence Agency.

Trump, for once, is most likely right. There is little hard evidence to back up Iran's claim. It is probably just another tactic in the escalating war of words and threats between this administration and Iran.

Furthermore, since the 1979 Iranian revolution and break in U.S.-Iran relations, American intelligence agencies have few if any ears and eyes on the ground in that country.

But this incident only highlights one of the most terrible — and costly — truths about Trump, his character, judgment, in fact, his entire presidency: Why should anyone believe him?

Trump has made false or misleading claims and comments 10,796 times since his inauguration, according to the Washington Post Fact Checker. From his documented ties to Russia to the border wall, on issues ranging from grave national security matters to his alleged sexual relations with porn stars and Playboy models, the president has shown time and again that he has not a shred of credibility.

Trump, a New York Times White House correspondent wrote recently, "has spun out so many misleading or untrue statements about himself, his enemies, his policies, his family, his personal story, his finances …that even his former communications director said 'he's a liar.'"

It is not only sad, but also extremely injurious to our national health and to our standing in the world.

There is reason to get tough on Iran. Iranian leaders are responsible for the deaths of hundreds of American soldiers during the war in Iraq. Their agents are considered responsible for the bombing of the U.S. Marine barracks in Beirut in 1983, which killed 240 Marines. Today, their proxies continue to exploit tensions across the Middle East.

The problem is that Trump has a very weak, second-rate national security team after getting rid of the first White House group because they didn't agree with him — with one reportedly calling him a "moron," and another saying that he has the mind of a "fifth- or sixth-grader."

As a result, combined with his total lack of credibility, the president has no real or long-term strategy for dealing with Iran. That has been painfully clear since he withdrew from the 2015 nuclear accord reached with Iran by President Barack Obama and China, Germany, France, Russia and Britain — who all still support the deal.

While constantly threatening fire and fury against Iran and its rulers, he has done nothing but back himself into a corner: not wanting war, supposedly, but unable to get

Tehran's leaders to agree to negotiate because he issued an ultimatum — a list of 12 demands, that no leader anywhere would accept.

Consequently, the Trump administration has allowed a mid-rank power, one that previously agreed not to pursue nuclear capability, to threaten to resume nuclear research, to endanger a crucial oil shipment route, and to gain the upper hand in a very dangerous confrontation.

In today's high-risk crisis, without credibility from many allies, Trump is not even respected by the Iranians, who do not seem to believe him when he threatens them. He has succeeded in isolating the U.S., not Iran.

If Trump had any sense of strategy, he could have doubled down on the 2015 nuclear agreement instead of withdrawing from it. Without increasing sanctions lifted under the accord, he could have demanded an end to provocative actions by Iranian proxies and curtailment of ballistic missile tests that continued. He could have intensified criticism of Iran's terrible human rights record.

One knowledgeable observer recently suggested a bold way for Trump to get himself and the United States out of a no-win position on Iran and its nuclear ambitions. Reese Erlich suggested a four-part stratagem: fire war-hawks like Secretary of State Mike Pompeo and National Security Adviser John Bolton, declare his "maximum pressure" campaign against Iran a great victory given clear damage to Iran's economy and oil exports, rejoin the 2015 nuclear agreement along with lifting sanctions, and sit down with

Iran's president to sort things out and seek a grand bargain. Though he's thus far accomplished nothing but 'photo ops,' that is virtually the same approach Trump has taken with North Korea, a country that already has a nuclear arsenal.

Part V. The Collapse of the Grand Old Party

The impeachment trial confirmed how far the Republican party has fallen into a pathetic throwback to the Know Nothing party of the 1840s and 1850s – one of several earlier parties that preceded the rise of the Grand Old Party.

Anti-immigrant fervor and xenophobia are shared by both the Know Nothings, the first major third party in American history, and today's Republican party.

The Know-Nothing party took its name from the pledge of its members to say "I know nothing" when asked for their beliefs. Not much different from so many Republicans today who, loyal to Trump, deny facts – such as how important immigrants have been and continue to be to this country.

Immigrants have been and continue to be major factors in almost all sectors of the American economy; former immigrants account for more than one-third of the Nobel prizes won by Americans.

As for the impeachment trial, all but one Republican senator ignored the weight of the evidence of Trump's abuse of power and almost uniform rejection of the need for witnesses and documents – cold-hard facts.

And what a stark contrast between the bold, honest and intelligent leader that emerged to lead the Republican party in the middle of the 19th century, Abraham Lincoln, and the vulgar, self-centered and unprincipled TV-reality star who presides over its 21st century shadow, Donald Trump.

But Trumpism has been enabled by a greedy, self-centered and bitterly partisan claque of power-hungry muldoons (Note # 4) in the Senate and House. Today's Republican party leaders are a sorry contrast to the wise, courageous and principled Republicans who led the party only a couple of decades ago – Richard Lugar, Charles Percy, Jacob Javits, Nancy Kassebaum, Howard Baker, Charles Mathias, etc.

Today's Republican Senate majority leader, Kentucky's Mitch McConnell, is a grasping, brown-nosing opportunist who proved his lack of interest in the health and welfare of the country when he said in 2012 that his No. 1 priority was to deny Barack Obama a second term. Not a word about the interests of the American people. Then his contemptible block on the Supreme Court nomination of Merrick Garland and later refusal to consider any legislation from the Democratic-controlled House in the 116th Congress. Nearly 400 pieces of legislation, on health care, infrastructure, gun control and protecting U.S. elections against Russian and other foreign interference, have been blocked by "Moscow" Mitch – so named for Russian investments in his impoverished state.

Other GOP leaders, senators Ted Cruz and Lindsay Graham and representatives such as Jim Jordan and Devin Nunes have proved themselves to be a timid collection of Trump toadies who place obeisance to Trump ahead of the country's interests and values. The constitutional design of checks and balances that are supposed to serve as a bulwark against authoritarian presidential power has been hurled out the window by these meek followers of the Trump cult.

The Republican party has been in steady moral decline since the arrival of Newt Gingrich and the "Tea Party" in the 1990s. The party that once stood for national security, fiscal discipline and civil rights is now a party that brought about the worst strategic decision in U.S. history (the Bush/Cheney invasion of Iraq), brought about the 2007-08 financial meltdown, backed a (Trump) tax cut for the 1 percent that sent the deficit through the roof, doesn't give a damn if 40 million Americans are without health care and seeks constantly to suppress voter turnout in elections.

****

The GOP reached its lowest point in the impeachment trial. All Republican senators except Mitt Romney of Utah held their noses and concluded that Trump's outrageous abuse of his power in pressuring Ukraine to investigate his likely 2020 rival was for a few, poor judgment, for most, just politics.

The ever-ambivalent Sen. Susan Collins of Maine uttered perhaps the most ridiculous defense of Trump when she said she thought Trump "has learned" from the scandal and would now be "more cautious." Within 24 hours, Trump trashed a National Prayer Breakfast to malign anyone who disagreed with him and fired career civil servants who testified against him.

Then in early 2020, Trump ignored multiple warnings about a possible pandemic, and two months after the coronavirus struck, many weeks after his own intelligence and public health agencies warned him of the gravity of the virus, called it a Democratic "hoax." He continued to deny, downplay and provide no decisive leadership to deal with the crisis as the American economy suffered its worst breakdown since the Depression. Incredibly, perhaps forgetting he is supposed to be the president, he said "I don't take any responsibility."

Ironically, Trump's awful response to Covid-19 cut the legs out from under the most positive development he could take some credit for: a strong economy.

Trump's shameful, scatter-brained performance prevented a successful approach to the pandemic, compounded by his administration's firing of many health and science experts and unwillingness to employ full-scale emergency powers to deal with it.

The Boston Globe captured the full picture accurately.

On April 3, 2020, as the number of deaths in the U.S. were climbing towards 50,000, the Globe commented: "The months the administration wasted with prevarications about the threat and its subsequent missteps will amount to exponentially more Covid-19 cases than were necessary. The President has blood on his hands."

His deep insecurity on display daily, Trump ranted at scientists and reporters, fired professional inspectors general who dared to criticize him, made baseless accusations that a critic had committed murder and flailed and flailed in a desperate attempt to rally his so-called base.

Unable to go to political rallies for a few months, he turned a daily White House briefing into a TV reality show during which he derided his own scientists and touted dangerous remedies such as injecting disinfectants and a highly unsafe drug.

Meanwhile the grave toll of deaths, so many of them unnecessary because of Trump's vanity and lack of leadership, continued to mount by July 15, 2020 to 135,000 – by far the worst in the world. The toll represented nearly 30 per cent of the deaths in the world, whereas the U.S. has less than five per cent of its population. Detailing the extent to which Trump had downsized the role of science, cut its budgetary outlays and even removed CDC agents in China where the virus first appeared, James Fallows in *The Atlantic* depicted an "irrational president," busy tweeting, as a pilot at the controls of America flying the country "straight into a mountainside."

Then the murder of a black man, George Floyd, in Minneapolis by a white policeman touched off days of largely peaceful protests across the country.

Once again, with an opportunity to calm deep tensions, to seek to unify the country, Trump opted to inflame divisions, using ugly military threats and force to promote his own political interests.

America's most respected generals and admirals, mostly Republican, condemned him as an immature man with little respect for the Constitution. Colin Powell, Secretary of State under George W. Bush, said Trump is a chronic liar who has undermined America's standing in the world and its most critical alliances. James Mattis, Trump's first Secretary of Defense, broke a long silence to excoriate Trump as divisive and incompetent, as did two former chairmen of the Joint Chiefs.

One of the most striking assessments came from a life-long Republican whose career spanned both the political and military worlds as a three-term senator and a secretary of defense and who, as a young member of Congress was one of the first Republican to stand up and call Richard Nixon to account for the Watergate scandal, William S. Cohen. In June 2020, citing Trump's actions, Cohen told CNN: "He is doing his best to tear down the institutions of the United States, to delegitimize the government and its generals. He is taking us down the road to tyranny."

Already amazed at how America had failed so dismally in dealing with the coronavirus response, the world now turned to disappointment and disgust at the United States under Donald Trump.

The European Union called for "swift resolution" of all the brutal injustices and inequities on display again in a warning used mainly for dictatorships and their rulers in the past. In a grim exclamation point of how far the United States had fallen in European regard, the EU said Americans are not welcome to travel there.

America under Trump – now a mockery of everything this country has stood for. The warning of the 50 leading Republican national security officials in August 2016, had come true: Donald Trump is indeed the most dangerous and reckless president in American history.

ARTICLES

Have Body Snatchers Invaded the GOP?
– The Baltimore Sun; May 21, 2019

Hollywood made several different versions of the classic science fiction horror film, "Invasion of the Body Snatchers," but some canny producers could be sizing up a new one. All they need to do is watch the scary remodeling of the Republican party under Donald Trump, especially the amazing conversion of once normal, pragmatic GOP senators and bureaucrats into obsequious, robot-like mouthpieces for Trumpian snake-oil.

Several GOP senators stand out as picture-perfect actors to play key roles, notably Lindsey Graham of South Carolina, Thom Tillis of North Carolina and Mitch McConnell of Kentucky.

To recall, "Invasion of the Body Snatchers" was a big screen hit movie in 1956 in which the people of a small town were being rapidly replaced by exact duplicates in the form of brain-dead, emotionless pods from outer space. A dramatic, spine-tingling film on its surface, many critics saw it as an allegory about the hysteria of the (Joseph) McCarthy period and the fascist rantings of the eventually disgraced Republican senator from Wisconsin.

A scene from the 1956 science fiction film, Invasion of the Body Snatchers, starring Dana Wynter and Kevin McCarthy.

Credit: The Everett Collection

Well, today, something very similar is happening to the Grand Old Party as so many of its members cave into the erratic, racist, constantly lying and wholly unprincipled presidency of Donald Trump. Nominations:

Best Actor in a Leading Role: Sen. Graham.

During the 2016 campaign, Senator Graham characterized Mr. Trump as "a jackass." He told interviewers Mr. Trump's "domestic and foreign policy is gibberish" and that Mr. Trump is "the most unprepared person I've ever met to be commander-in-chief."

Today, Senator Graham is Mr. Trump's leading toady on Capitol Hill, repeatedly defending the president's reckless abuse of power, his constant lies and 180-degree switchbacks on foreign policy. Senator Graham's complete conversion is reflected in his willingness to ignore the massive Russian interference in the 2016 election along with the president's demeaning of his supposed best friend, John McCain.

Best Supporting Actor: Sen. Tillis.

Senator Tillis excoriated President Trump in The Washington Post two months ago for his declaration of a national emergency over a border wall as an abuse of executive power. A few days later, he voted with Mr. Trump.

Honorable mention: Senator McConnell

Senator McConnell is a strong contender for this award. The majority leader who famously said his No. 1 goal was to keep Barack Obama from gaining a second term instead of promoting the national interest, has been ridiculed by Mr. Trump and called a failure. Yet, with his re-election upcoming, he now salutes and surrenders his integrity and American governance to Trumpian whims.

Best Adapted Screenplay: Attorney General William Barr.

Mr. Barr served as A.G. under George H.W. Bush, compiling a respectable record as the nation's overseer of law and justice.

Today, instead of performing his constitutional duties, Mr. Barr has become a virtual echo chamber for Mr. Trump, repeating his chant of "no collusion, no collusion" like a parrot when there are actually many instances of collusion and obstruction in the Mueller report — just not enough to prosecute a president.

Mr. Barr's rush to judgment with a misleading four-page summary of the report has now been criticized by Special Counsel Robert Mueller as not accurately reflecting the substance of the investigations and multiple episodes of obstruction by Mr. Trump and his acolytes.

There are dozens of other such empty suits in Washington taking over the party of Abraham Lincoln these days. They mimic Mr. Trump's suggestion that climate change is "a Chinese hoax." They twist themselves into contortions to support a tax cut that sent the deficit through the roof. They show up at Trump rallies and still chant "lock her up" even though it's Mr. Trump's associates who are the convicted felons.

The director of a 1978 remake of "Body Snatchers," Philip Kaufman, sees a frightening parallel between the end of his movie and Trump rallies of today — especially when Mr. Trump, employing a favorite Stalinist phrase, turns on the press as "the enemy of the people."

"The way Trump points to the press at the back of the auditorium and everybody turns (to jeer at reporters), you get that scary, 'poddy' feeling," Mr. Kaufman told The Hollywood Reporter. "There's a kind of contagion that's going on here."

Who said "truth is stranger than fiction?" They're both strange in this case.

Trump: 'Inept,' 'Clumsy' and Above All 'Insecure' – *The Baltimore Sun; July 16, 2019*

British ambassador Kim Darroch said the White House under President Donald Trump is "inept," "clumsy," "uniquely dysfunctional" and could collapse in "disgrace."

So, what else is new? Sir Kim — "an extraordinarily effective" representative of British interests — decided to resign after these comments were made public, despite support from his government. A shame; he said nothing that much of the world doesn't already know. Donald J. Trump is "inept," "clumsy," and "uniquely dysfunctional," to put it mildly.

Mr. Darroch's analysis is dead right. Just take stock: The truth is staring us in the face every single day - from Donald Trump's constant lies and attacks on the rule of law and the press; to backward policies on everything from climate change to health care; to unprecedented corruption and many jail-bound cronies; to his reckless, erratic foreign policy, which has accomplished nothing except bringing us closer to a disastrous war.

We can't say we were not warned. In 2016, 50 of the most respected Republican leaders on national security declared that Donald Trump, if elected, would be "the most reckless president in American history."

The group included former CIA director Michael Hayden; Robert Zoellick, the deputy secretary of state for President Reagan; and two former directors of homeland security. Leading conservatives like George Will and Eliot Cohen have condemned President Trump as incompetent.

But Mr. Darroch's assessment included one more description that has been a bit lost in the tumult: that Donald Trump is "insecure."

Lack of judgment, lack of character, lack of experience, lack of integrity and many other shortcomings have been laid at the president's doorstep. Not many have mentioned insecurity.

Yet, telltale evidence of this character flaw has been there from the very beginning. Within hours of his inauguration, the new president was on a warpath when news accounts reported that the crowds in attendance were significantly smaller than Barack Obama's. Soon, Mr. Trump ranted about illegal voters and "immigrants" to suggest that his 3 million vote defeat by Hillary Clinton in the popular vote was rigged (No rigging was found).

Overseeing the first full meeting of his new Cabinet, Mr. Trump rambled on about his many "accomplishments" in his first months in office. Despite achieving little, even with Republican control of Congress, the new president went around the room to seek reassurance from each Cabinet secretary.

One by one, they groveled, offering high praise for the president. Health Secretary Tom Price, soon gone for abuse of office, spoke of Mr. Trump's "great leadership," while Commerce Secretary Wilbur Ross, reportedly on the outs over his Census immigration question rationale, went on about "the thrill" he felt helping the president deliver on his campaign promises.

Only Gen. James Mattis, then secretary of defense, had the courage to finesse Mr. Trump's desperate search for flattery.

General Mattis paid tribute to the men and women of the armed forces.

Just this spring, Mr. Trump engaged in a re-run of this flattery show, calling on five aides to describe his "demeanor" after a White House collision with Democratic leaders. "Very calm," "very calm," they chirped.

Other signs of Mr. Trump's insecurity abound. He fires senior officials by "tweet" rather than face them in person. He calls himself "a stable genius" but refuses to release his grades. He terms himself a billionaire but won't release his tax returns. He spends as much as 60% of his day in "executive time" — largely watching television to see how he is being covered.

He is afraid to hold a real press conference — a serious encounter where he would have to think fast, prove he can react with something more than mono-syllabic attacks and insults. He prefers to meet reporters next to helicopters; with engines roaring, he can shout down or walk away from tough questions.

Experts on handwriting see insecurity in the president's signature. A Pittsburgh expert, Michelle Dresbold, characterizes his angular, up and down scrawl as reflecting a person who is "aggressive, angry, fearful, rigid and uptight."

The timing of Ambassador Darroch's analysis is propitious, coming a few days after the 45th president hijacked a non-partisan national holiday to try to bolster his flagging popularity.

And why? Because Donald J. Trump is, at bottom, terribly insecure.

Ratcliffe Represents Trump's Third – and Third-rate – National Security Team – *The Dallas Morning News* with James Goodby; August 1, 2019

The first team of national security leaders for President Donald Trump has come and gone, in part due to criminal activity, in part because they told Trump real truths about critical international challenges that he didn't want to hear.

Michael Flynn departed after pleading guilty to lying about contacts with Russians. His successor, Gen. H.R. McMaster, and Secretary of State Rex Tillerson were tweeted out for not sufficiently kowtowing to Trump. Secretary of Defense Gen. James Mattis left after Trump ignored his advice on the president's off-the-cuff decisions on withdrawal of troops from Syria and U.S.-South Korea military exercises.

All of these initial choices, except Flynn, were considered highly capable, experienced leaders, with respect for acting in the national interest — not the politics of Trump. They took their oath of office and the mission of their respective roles seriously.

Then came the second team, headed by a partisan secretary of state, Michael Pompeo, who has said God chose Trump to protect the state of Israel, and national security adviser John Bolton, who wants to bomb Iran and North Korea, yet ducked regular military service because he "did not want to die in a Southeast Asia rice paddy."

Now comes a third team of third-raters. To replace Dan Coats, a respected former Republican senator, as director of national intelligence, Trump has chosen a former mayor of a city of 10,000 in Texas, John Ratcliffe, a congressman who has hardly any experience in intelligence and diplomacy.

Last spring, Coats had the temerity to offer clear-eyed intelligence Trump did not want to hear: that North Korea is still considered a nuclear threat, that ISIS has not been "defeated," that Iran has been abiding by its commitment to the 2015 nuclear agreement, and that Russia did undertake massive interference in the 2016 presidential election. Coats also declined to investigate Trump's false claim that President Barack Obama had "spied" on him.

Director of national intelligence is a very serious job. Without significant power, it demands an extraordinary combination of moral integrity, truth-telling and devotion to the best interests of the nation.

There have been only five directors of national intelligence since the position was created after 9/11. The first was a distinguished career diplomat, the next three were senior officers with extensive experience in intelligence. The fifth,

Coats, Trump's appointee, was the first politician. Let's remember why the job was created.

The 9/11 Commission laid heavy emphasis on the failures of the FBI and the CIA to keep each other informed and also on the lack of imagination among senior leaders in foreseeing the terrorist attacks of al-Qaeda. The bipartisan commission concluded that President George W. Bush (and predecessors) was poorly served by the institutions that had been created after World War ll to prevent another Pearl Harbor.

One of their remedies was to realign the intelligence community in a way that would end the parochialism that had led to stove-piping of important information, which led to intelligence failures with disastrous consequences. Distorted intelligence about Iraq's nuclear capability led to the invasion of Iraq, a poor strategic decision.

So the director of national intelligence is one of the most critical positions in the U.S. government. Oddly, it has little command authority. The position was not established to supersede the responsibilities of the directors of the FBI, the CIA, and the other intelligence agencies but was directed to contribute the vision, imagination and ability to insist on the integration of intelligence and to have it implemented.

It is one reason why the position requires a balanced, almost apolitical leader, to herd cats. Above all, it is why it's so important Trnt for the U.S. Senate to consider whether any nominee has the rather unique qualifications to do the job.

Failure to do the job well could be calamitous to the ultimate safety and survival of our country.

(Author's note: After stiff criticism from both parties, President Trump withdrew the Ratcliffe nomination one day after this article appeared. He renamed Ratcliffe several months later for the same position, and his appointment was confirmed by a narrow partisan majority despite continuing recognition of his lack of qualifications.)

Senate Should Not Ram Through Impeachment Trial
– *The Baltimore Sun*; December 30, 2019

Virtually all experts and observers envision a near-certain acquittal of President Donald Trump by the U. S. Senate after the House passage of two articles of impeachment Dec. 18th.

The Constitution requires a vote of two-thirds of the Senate to convict and remove a president — or 67 votes. However damning and culpable Mr. Trump's actions in withholding critical aid to Ukraine against Russian aggression to force an investigation of a political rival, very few believe that 20 Republican senators will join 45 Democrats and two Independents likely to vote for conviction.

But the larger, and perhaps more important question is whether the trial is going to be conducted fairly, with full respect for the Constitution and the rule of law.

Mitch McConnell, the Republican Senate majority leader, has already placed a heavy hand on the scales against a fair trial. He said he will work closely with the White House to oversee the trial, though his control over the trial is limited. The Constitution places the chief justice of the Supreme Court, John Roberts, as the presiding officer — not Mr. McConnell.

But Mr. McConnell's strong bias in favor of what amounts to an indicted defendant, President Trump, is equal to having the head of a jury say he will side with the defendant before a trial even begins.

The ranking Senate Democrat, Chuck Schumer, wrote to Mr. McConnell, urging him to guarantee a fair trial in the interests of all parties and the country. That would mean, Mr. Schumer wrote, the appearance of key White House officials who have refused to testify and the release of vital documents withheld by the president.

There are several Republican senators who do not like or respect Mr. Trump — and are not afraid to say so. They range from outspoken critics like Mitt Romney (Utah) to occasionally independent skeptics such as Lisa Murkowski (Alaska), Susan Collins (Maine) and Pat Toomey (Pennsylvania).

While many more quietly express disdain for Mr. Trump, his policies and behavior, it totals far less than 20, barring a bombshell soon.

Yet, along with 47 Democrats and Independents, it would take just four senators to block Mr. McConnell's drive to ram through a verdict without calling key witnesses and hidden documents. A 51-49 vote to require those witnesses and documents, including a full, un-redacted version of the Ukraine call, would bring those to account.

Mr. Trump's refusal to allow key White House officials to testify and to release vital documents is tantamount to Richard Nixon's cover-up in 1974 — the key act that led to his approaching impeachment and resignation. Even Mr. Nixon did not block White House officials from testifying.

The American public has a right to hear from White House officials who refused to testify before the House of Representatives as they developed two articles of impeachment, for abuse of power and obstruction of Congress. They are, especially, Secretary of State Mike Pompeo, acting chief of staff Mick Mulvaney, and former national security adviser, John Bolton, who was fired by Mr. Trump. Mr. Bolton once objected to the Ukraine meddling by Mr. Trump's personal lawyer Rudy Giuliani as "a drug deal."

The near-total acceptance of Mr. Trump's behavior by virtually all Republicans to this point is shameful. In addition to turning a blind eye to Russian aggression in Ukraine, basically supporting Vladimir Putin, the

Republican party has ignored an unprecedented pattern of corruption and unlawful behavior by Mr. Trump and his close aides.

Mr. Trump fired or castigated anyone who dared to oppose him, from Assistant Attorney General Sally Yates, who warned about the Russian connections of then national security adviser Michael Flynn, to James Comey to Michael Cohen. Cohen paid $130,000 in hush money to a porn star to help Trump. Flynn pled guilty; Mr. Cohen is in jail.

Paul Manafort, Mr. Trump's campaign manager, is serving a seven-year jail term for corrupt activities. The favoritism shown Mr. Trump's children by China, Arab countries and others is far worse than GOP claims against the Bidens.

Once Democratic House managers of impeachment lay out their case, the only defense for Trumpite Republicans is to try to slam the door on revelation of the broader context of a truly "deep state" of malfeasance and corruption embodied by the 45th president. Even the vice-presidential option to break a 50-50 tie on demands for critical witnesses and documents would fail if four Republican senators stood up for justice and the rule of law.

It's Hard to Deny that Russia is Benefiting from Trump
– *The Dallas Morning News* with Col. Sam Gardiner; January 28, 2020

A most pertinent comment relevant to the spotlight on Donald J. Trump, the 45th president of the United States, only the third president to be impeached, came 232 years ago at the founding of the republic.

In 1788, Alexander Hamilton penned this brilliant comment in Federalist No. 68, the articles that framed our exceptional Constitution.

Noting that every obstacle was needed to prevent interference by foreign powers, then thought to be Britain and France, Hamilton wrote: "These most deadly adversaries of republican government might naturally have been expected to make their approaches from more than one quarter, but chiefly from the desire in foreign powers to gain an improper ascendant in our councils (of government). How could they better gratify this than by raising a creature of their own to the chief magistracy of the Union."

On Jan. 22, Rep. Jason Crow, D-Colo., brought the dangers of foreign influence into stark personal focus when he stood in the Senate and outlined an accusation of how Trump blocked U.S. military aid for Ukraine in its struggle against Russian aggression to pressure the government of Ukraine to interfere in American politics — for Trump's political benefit.

Crow, a decorated Army Ranger in Iraq and Afghanistan, described how Trump's holdup of this vital aid coincided with the death of a courageous 38-year-old Ukrainian soldier, Oleksandr Markiv.

According to the *Los Angeles Times*, Markiv was fatally wounded while fighting off Russian mercenaries, not long after Trump's July 25 phone call with the Ukrainian leader. Crow's recounting of the *Times* article on the condition of Ukrainian soldiers in their fight against Russia was compelling.

Crow also described how he and fellow Rangers in Iraq salvaged scrap metal to deal with roadside bombs because they were poorly equipped — even by U. S. standards in 2003. He contrasted that experience with how Markiv and thousands of patriotic Ukrainians fought without boots and bullets against well-armed Russian forces.

"So, when we talk about troops not getting equipment they need, it's personal to me," Crow said. "Real people's lives are at stake. That's why this matters."

Crow then noted the many respected diplomats and military leaders who testified about the need to help our allies in Europe, that Ukraine is a friend, and that Russia remains a foe. Crow concluded: "Who here will be on the right side of history?"

Not Republican senators, it seems, if they continue to fear and protect Donald Trump, a man who openly admires

Russian leader Vladimir Putin and takes Putin's word over American intelligence agencies.

The focus of the impeachment trial is on presidential abuse of power and obstruction of Congress in Trump's now well-documented decisions to block that aid to Ukraine until he could force Ukraine's leaders into investigating the Bidens, a direct invitation to intervene in America.

There are two other issues of great consequence in this trial. One is the brutal Russian aggression in Ukraine.

Another is Trump's repeated ignorance and insults of the role of professional diplomats, intelligence officials and military leaders in protecting U.S. national security.

It started during the 2016 campaign, with his savage maligning of the war record of the late John McCain and his boast that he knows "more about ISIS than the generals." He compared U.S. intelligence agencies with Nazi Germany, and one by one, once in the White House, fired all the generals he named to senior posts because they challenged his decisions and impulsive decision-making. He repeatedly has attacked professional diplomats.

A new book, *A Very Stable Genius: Donald J. Trump's Testing of America*, by Philip Rucker and Carol Leonnig, reveals that during a serious 2017 briefing on national security with the Joint Chiefs of Staff, Trump, who avoided military service due to "bone spurs," called our leading generals and admirals "a bunch of dopes and babies" and said in anger, "You're all losers. ... You don't know how to win anymore."

It was after this meeting that then-Secretary of State Rex Tillerson, whose father and grandfather had been combat veterans, said about Trump: "He's a [expletive] moron."

This is a president?

<u>Write in William Weld to Send a Message to the Republican Party</u>
<u>– *Bangor Daily News*; February 28, 2020</u>

Bipartisanship in Congress has vanished as American democracy in the days of Donald Trump has suffered a dramatic collision of polarized political division. But it was not always that way.

In 1986, despite the same 47-53 minority as today, Democratic senators proposed a sweeping set of sanctions to press for real change in the white minority government of South Africa, then a pariah on the world stage.

Two moderate Republican senators, Charles "Mac" Mathias Jr. of Maryland, and Daniel Evans of Washington, took the lead in convincing Democratic colleagues, including Joseph Biden, to drop harsher provisions, such as closing the U.S. Embassy and blocking South African Airways from flying to the United States.

Mathias and Evans argued that such measures would cut off communications and intelligence gathering in an important country and hurt the United States. They agreed to back key Democratic measures such as stiff economic sanctions, an end to arms sales and a demand to free Nelson Mandela — then in jail — who later was the leader of the country.

As a result, a strong bipartisan bill was put together. Senate Foreign Relations Committee Chairman Richard Lugar, a Republican, then backed the bill. The legislation was approved by the Senate, but vetoed by President Ronald Reagan.

Yet, 31 Republicans, including a first-term Kentucky senator named Mitch McConnell, joined the Democrats to override Reagan's veto by a vote of 78-21. McConnell said Reagan's policy of "constructive engagement" was "wrong."

Many factors led the white minority government in South Africa to surrender the reins of government to the black majority in the early 1990s. But the principled — and bipartisan — opposition of the United States played a key role.

Mathias and Evans were truly moderate senators who knew how to act in the national interest — a state of political courage and compromise that does not exist in today's Republican Party.

Today, the GOP has become a pale shadow of its own history. It is in thrall to an intemperate, narcissistic and reckless demagogue who has no deep convictions other than what is good for his ego and pocketbook.

Under Trump, the party of Lincoln no longer supports civil and voting rights. Once considered the party of national security, the GOP now backs a president who supports Russia, a designated enemy. Once considered the party of fiscal discipline, it is now the party that ignores a sky-high deficit that followed Trump's tax cut for the 1 percent.

Few Republicans dare to stand up to Trump, a former TV reality star who does not respect American values and the rule of law. He maligns top generals and admirals as "babies," "dopes" and "losers"; he tells hangers-on to " take out" respected diplomats; and he regularly takes the word of an authoritarian Russian leader over American intelligence agencies.

The Republican Party under Trump today shows little interest in bipartisan cooperation to tackle critical issues. With the exception of progress on criminal justice reform, the GOP today has moved to overturn health care, environmental standards and moderate gun measures. The Senate, under McConnell, has refused to act on nearly 400 bills passed by the House, including critical bills on infrastructure, climate change, and protecting our elections from Russian interference again.

Despite occasional murmurs of objection, Sen. Susan Collins, the last Republican in Congress from New England, has mostly gone along with the Trump- and McConnell-led destruction of bipartisanship.

Maine voters will soon decide on whether Collins deserves re-election. Meanwhile, despite only one name on the Republican ballot in Maine for the March 3 presidential primary, voters do have an option besides Trump.

You can write in a candidate, although that vote won't be counted. And there is a strong, moderate Republican candidate who deserves support of every Republican who believes the party needs to return to the party of Lincoln, not remain Trump's plaything.

William Weld was an effective governor of Massachusetts for two terms. He is an articulate, savvy lawyer who worked on the impeachment inquiry against Richard Nixon.

As a resident of Maine, a Republican and a person who is concerned about a rudderless, reckless and unprincipled president, I plan to write in William Weld in the March 3 primary in Maine.

<u>The Cost of Trump's Denial, Delay and Indecisive Leadership</u>
<u>– *Bath Brunswick Times-Record/Portland Press Herald;* April 9, 2020</u>

The hundreds and hundreds of Donald Trump's lies and distortions of the truth and his utter lack of leadership are

coming home to roost in the deadly spread of a novel virus
he ignored for far too long.

Trump's repeated denial, downplaying, now indecisive
leadership over the last three months have wreaked grave
havoc on this nation's readiness and ability to deal with this
terrible disease.

It did not have to be this way, dozens of health and science
experts, agree.

Two months after the outbreak in China, a month after his
own intelligence agencies warned of the serious risk of the
virus reaching our shores, Donald Trump told a rally in
South Carolina that Democratic criticism of him and his
failure to recognize the gravity of the threat was "their
hoax." That was February 28, 2020. One month earlier, his
top trade advisor had warned the White House the virus
could cost more than one million American lives and shatter
the economy if aggressive action was not taken.

Before and since, Trump has issued one false, misleading or
dead-wrong claim after another – while failing to provide
steady, confidence-building leadership.

"We have it totally under control." January 22.

"When it gets a little warmer, it miraculously goes away."
February 10.

"The coronavirus is very much under control in the USA.
Stock market looks very good." February 24.

"We have only 15 cases." February 26.

"I felt it was a pandemic long before it was a pandemic."
March 17.

Saying "we can't let the cure be worse than the problem,"
Trump said, "you'll have packed churches all over the
country (on Easter)." March 24.

It was not until March 13 that Trump ordered a national
emergency. The National Response Framework, set up to
deal with all major disasters, to prepare for everything from
nuclear war to terror attacks, could have been deployed
weeks before. He still has not employed full powers of the
Defense Production Act, to command manufacture of tests,
masks, ventilators and other critical equipment. Instead of
acting like a commander-in-chief of a nation, he now
restricts usage of the federal stockpile.

Incredibly, reversing Harry Truman's commitment that "the
buck stops here," Trump said "I take no responsibility" for
the administration's terribly costly response.

Months too late, with grudging recognition of the crisis,
Donald J. Trump is beginning to realize that the coronavirus
crisis is not another TV reality show.

Yet after saying a few kind words about Democratic
governors in California, New York and Washington state –
all battling the worst outbreaks – he soon reverted to form,
telling governors he does not like not to call for federal help.

The president's denial and stumbling recognition of a grave threat to our national security is the direct result of Trump's inability – and in fact, outright opposition – to run an open, fact-based administration since 2016.

A few more facts:

Fact: A full-scale simulation by the administration's Department of Health and Human Services in mid-2019 highlighted the grave risk of a pandemic and warned that major steps were critical to prepare. Its October 2019 report projected 586,000 Americans would die.

Fact: In three-plus years, Trump and his minions have taken a broadsword to science and health programs. He severely weakened the office of national security adviser, downsizing its health emergency staff. His administration has wiped out major environmental regulations and reduced funds for the Center for Disease Control and the World Health Organization.

Trump's abiding disdain for anyone who disagrees with him is strikingly evident in three blatant actions in the last month – all appalling during a national crisis.

A loyal, inexperienced crony is firing respected officers in the intelligence community deemed critical of Trump. Trump has fired several professional inspector generals.

Second, today when national unity is essential, Trump continues to engage in conspiracy theories. He still attacks the "deep state," professional experts we need in any crisis. It is "the Chinese virus."

Third, Trump continues to malign the media. During the crisis, he has renewed attacks on "the enemy of the people," – the favorite phrase of Soviet dictator, Joseph Stalin.

Yet, during this crisis, it is newspapers, television networks and other outlets whose reporters and editors have risen brilliantly to the challenge and provided outstanding information and analysis.

It is the most sinister of ironies that this narcissistic president, a former TV reality star who campaigned on "Make America Great Again" continues to show in the most severe national security crisis in decades that he has very little concern for anyone but himself.

<u>Why Can't Trump Be More Like FDR?</u>
<u>– *The Baltimore Sun;* June 16, 2020</u>

Shortly after the attack on Pearl Harbor, Eleanor Roosevelt, a dynamic first lady, flew from Washington to the West Coast as co-leader of the Office of Civilian Defense to assure Americans of steadfast help in the coming crisis.

In Los Angeles, the president's wife told state leaders: "I came here to find out from you what are the most helpful things we in Washington can do to help you. Tell me what you found lacking and what you want," according to "No

Ordinary Time," by Doris Kearns Goodwin, a remarkable history of the Roosevelts and the homefront in World War II.

Many weeks after his own intelligence agencies warned of a deadly threat to the United States from the coronavirus outbreak in China, President Donald Trump called the virus the Democrat's "hoax" at a political rally. Several days after the first Americans had died in California and the state of Washington, Mr. Trump called the governor of Washington "a snake" and continued to downplay the gravity of the virus.

One day after the Japanese attack at Pearl Harbor, President Franklin D. Roosevelt went before Congress and delivered a brief, inspiring speech to rally the country and to declare that December 7, 1941 would "live in infamy."

For days and weeks as more Americans began to contract COVID-19 and die, Donald Trump continued to downplay the threat of contagion. He said it was "only 15 people," it "is going to go away" — like "a miracle."

One month after Pearl Harbor, in his State of the Union address, FDR outlined a staggering set of production goals for industry for 1942: 60,000 planes, 45,000 tanks, six million tons of merchant ships — in a year. That translated into a plane every four minutes, a tank every seven minutes, two sea-going ships a day.

When warned before that speech that American industry —
long held back by isolationist-minded "America Firsters" —
could not meet such goals, FDR doubled the initial figures.

Donald Trump has failed to even use the full powers of the
federal government, available in the Defense Production Act
and other laws, to combat the virus.

While countries such as South Korea and Germany promptly
ordered widespread testing and other critical equipment
that dramatically limited the spread of the virus, Mr. Trump
has claimed the federal government is not a "shipping clerk"
and vowed to block supplies to states whose governors
criticized him. He said he takes "no responsibility" for the
overall response to the worst attack on the security and
health of the United States since World War II.

The contrast between Donald Trump and FDR is stark, and
all glaringly evident from Ms. Goodwin's book.

FDR's leadership, so effective in dealing with the Depression
in his first two terms, stands out as that of a smart,
self-confident — even if severely crippled — leader with no
fear for his political future. In contrast, Donald Trump has
proved to be exactly what many observers — including
Republicans — feared he would be: a waffling, unstable
narcissist whose overriding concern is his own political fate.

And it is not just in the United States — which with more
than 116,000 deaths has around 27% of the world's deaths

from coronavirus when we have 4.25% of its population —
that Mr. Trump's lack of leadership has proved devastating.
His administration has sought to blame anyone but itself for
the haphazard U.S. response, starting with China, whose
leaders do bear responsibility for an initial cover-up. Mr.
Trump has ended funding for the World Health
Organization; he has blocked international aid to Iran — a
country with which he seeks to provoke conflict. His
administration refused to join an international search for
effective vaccines.

Today, Mr. Trump critics and cartoonists are having a field
day with his lack of leadership, contempt for bipartisanship,
insecurity and lack of compassion. Sadly, truth is as strange
as fiction — and the most damning portrayals of the 45th
president are not outlandish, such as Mr. Trump's serious
suggestion of injecting disinfectant as a cure.

Donald Trump needs to place the country's health and
security above his political future.

Near the end of the 2016 campaign, 50 leading Republican
experts on national security warned that Mr. Trump, if
elected, would prove to be "the most dangerous" and "most
reckless" president in American history.

Mr. Trump's die-hard base may not like it, but the evidence
is becoming clear that those leaders, including directors of
the CIA and Homeland Security under George W. Bush,
knew what they were talking about.

<u>**Why it Matters That Military Leaders are Speaking Out Against Trump**</u>
<u>*— Bangor Daily News; June 12, 2020*</u>

Just three years ago, one memorable image from Donald Trump's first full Cabinet meeting stands out in stark relief to explain why the eruption of criticism of the president today poses a grave threat to his presidency.

With television cameras rolling on June 12, 2017, Trump went around the table and solicited statements from the officials. With one exception, they all bestowed elaborate praise on Trump.

Vice President Mike Pence said it was "the greatest privilege of my life" to serve Trump. Nikki Haley, the new ambassador to the United Nations, chimed in, "We're back," as if the U.S. had just vanished in the past decade.

Secretary of Defense Gen. James Mattis, sitting next to Trump, simply said, "It is an honor to represent the men and women of the Department of Defense, and we are grateful for the sacrifices our people are making in order to strengthen our military as far as diplomatic, we always negotiate from a position of strength."

In other words, there was one person with self-respect in the room.

It was a significant sign of times to come. With the exception of Mattis, all of these Cabinet members have remained sycophantic supporters of Donald Trump, quit under the shadow of ethics violations or departed because of policy differences.

Mattis remained in the revolving door of the Trump administration longer than most. Despite deep disagreements with Trump over major national security issues, Mattis stayed on until Trump made a series of impulsive decisions on U.S. troops in Syria and a unilateral suspension of U.S. military exercises with South Korea to please North Korea's dictator.

And that is why Mattis' withering critique of Trump's reckless use of military force against peaceful protests in Washington signals a perilous moment in the presidency of Donald Trump.

Trump has no one to blame but himself. It was Trump who opted to exploit the nationwide protests and racial tensions after the murder of George Floyd in Minneapolis instead of seeking to unify the country — already tense due to the pandemic. It was Trump, and his attorney general, William Barr, who hoodwinked their current defense secretary, Mark Esper, and Joint Chiefs of Staff Chairman Mark Milley into a march across Lafayette Square so Trump could hold a photo-op in front of a church. Milley has since said he should not have been there and hundreds of West Point graduates criticized the politicization of the military in a letter to the academy's 2020 graduates.

That ugly scene, with American military forces and police battering their way through demonstrators, has fueled intense criticism of Trump.

Nearly 300 retired military and diplomatic officers signed a letter condemning the Trump administration for its heavy-handed response to the protests.

The most damning criticism came from the most respected military leaders.

Breaking a long silence, Mattis wrote, "Donald Trump is the first president in my lifetime who does not try to unite the American people — does not even pretend to try. Instead he tries to divide us. We are witnessing the consequences of three years without mature leadership."

Adm. Mike Mullen, a former chairman of the Joint Chiefs, said Trump "laid bare his disdain for the rights of peaceful protest, and risked politicizing the men and women of our armed forces."

Colin Powell, a general and secretary of state in the Bush administration, called Trump a chronic liar whose reckless

policies have done irreparable damage to America's
alliances and standing in the world.

Such stark criticism of a president by senior military leaders
is highly unusual. But Trump, a recipient of questionable
draft exemptions, has been very clumsy in his treatment of
senior military leaders — and shown disrespect for a
time-honored relationship between military leaders and
their elected civilian leaders, even calling top generals
"dopes and babies."

Despite claiming he knew "more than the generals" during
the 2016 campaign, he appointed many generals and
admirals to leading positions in the government. All have
quit — in open disagreement with or contempt for the
president's whimsical decision-making.

Relations between presidents and their military leaders have
often been difficult; note the Truman-MacArthur
confrontation, differences during the Vietnam War, the
failure to listen to military objections to the invasion of Iraq.
But the scale and character of today's collision between a
president and his top commanders, highlighted by Trump's
misuse of the military and open disdain for its leaders, is a
sharp break with the past and places the country on a
dangerous path.

Nixon and Trump: Where is Barry Goldwater When We Really Need Him?
– Bath Brunswick Times-Record (Portland Press Herald); August 10, 2020

In the year 1974, it took seven months for the dam to break and flood the presidency of Richard Milhous Nixon.

In January 1974, many Republican senators and representatives became well aware of the mounting evidence of abuse of office and the disintegrating stonewall that Nixon and his minions had erected around the 37th president.

As evidence of Nixon's lying, cover-up and abuse of the country's institutions were being uncovered by the Washington Post and other news outlets, a conservative Republican congressman from New York, Barber Conable, wrote in his diary that "it's hard to think of (Nixon) without revulsion, not because I consider him loathsome, but because I consider him incredibly stupid as a leader."

Despite that spreading view of Nixon, it took seven more months, upstanding courage from seven Republicans on the House Judiciary Committee and release of the Watergate tapes before three Republican leaders summoned the courage to go to the White House, and tell Nixon: "GO."

That was 46 years ago this week. On August 7, 1974, Sen. Barry Goldwater, a GOP icon from Arizona and two colleagues visited the White House a few weeks after release of the explosive "smoking gun" tape in which Nixon and top aide H. R. Haldeman agreed on a plan to tell the FBI to stop the investigation (of the break-in at Democratic headquarters).

Nixon resigned 36 hours after the visit from Goldwater and his colleagues, effective at noon, Aug. 9, 1974.

There are many parallels and many differences between the political conditions then and today. But there is no doubt that the presidency of Donald John Trump is in dire straits in 2020 after three and a half years of little accomplishment, repeated trampling on the rule of law, attempts to shred U.S. alliances and now five months of the most disastrous failure of leadership in modern American history.

Richard Nixon faced three counts of impeachment, including obstruction of justice and abuse of power. Trump survived impeachment due to the complete absence today of the bipartisanship and conscience of the 1970s Republicans – who placed national interest above party.

That's the major difference. Like their predecessors, Republican lawmakers today are Jello-like nervous behind the scenes about Trump's reckless behavior and abysmal leadership. But they are shaking in their boots about how to deal with that reality.

The predicament of the country today is far worse than it was in 1974. For all his faults, Nixon did pursue pragmatic policies abroad, including the opening to China, détente with the Soviet Union, historic nuclear weapons treaties and, at home, establishment of the Environmental Protection Agency.

Trump has accomplished virtually nothing, except two Supreme Court justices, hardly a feat with GOP Senate control, and a tax cut that did nothing but enrich the 1 percent and skyrocket the deficit.

Now, after nearly a full term, the United States is suffering from a grave pandemic that Trump and his administration first ignored, calling it a Democratic "hoax," then pursued self-centered policies aimed only at his reelection. Meanwhile, as many other developed countries reduced the threat from Covid-19 by tough action and smart prevention, 150,000 Americans have died – 25 per cent of the world total when the U.S. has less than five per cent of its population.

Yet after cutting science and health programs, Trump is now openly insulting the nation's leading health experts, such as Dr. Anthony Fauci, suing to overturn the Affordable (Health) Care Act and is even raising doubt that he would leave the White House if defeated in November.

Barry Goldwater and friends, where are you? Senate majority leader Mitch McConnell and leaders like Senators Ted Cruz and Lindsay Graham are afraid of their shadow, like all Republicans except Mitt Romney. And there is a smoking gun: the deaths of 150,000 Americans who have died because of Trump's failure to uphold his oath "to preserve, protect and defend the Constitution of the United States."

As the Trump presidency spirals downward, as he tells Republican governors to "reopen" only to find staggering surges in COVID-19, as he seeks desperately to repress voting, as he dispatches secret government police to pose as Mr. "law and order," the looming question of the day is:

Who is going to come forward in the next weeks to tell Trump to return to the world of real estate and reality television – to resign? The tricky part might be to find a way to grant a pardon for any future prosecution, both on federal and state levels.

But the overarching question remains. Who is going to say the dam is breaking, the water is reaching flood stage? Who is ready to pull the plug on a failed presidency?

<u>Most of the World Dislikes Trump | Commentary</u>
<u>– *The Baltimore Sun; October 21, 2020*</u>

"When in the course of human events, it becomes necessary for one people to dissolve the political bands ... a decent respect to the opinions of mankind requires that they should declare the causes which impel them to the separation."
— Declaration of Independence, 1776.

Respect for the United States across the world has registered a predictable pattern of highs and lows in rough convergence with the successes and failures of various administrations in the modern era.

Certainly the World War II period and the brief end of the 20th century "hyperpower" reign after the collapse of the Soviet Union stand out as the apex of respect and actual predominance.

Alternatively, the late 1960s and early 1970s during the Vietnam War and racial turmoil at home, along with the disastrous invasion of Iraq in 2003, mark low points in international opinion of America.

But nothing compares with the damage that President Donald Trump has done to the standing and image of this country in four years as president.

A recent international opinion poll underlines how Mr. Trump's "Make America Great Again" campaign has become "Make America Alone" in the world — and brought respect for the United States to a historic low point.

The Pew Research Center surveyed 13,273 people in 13 countries — all friendly nations in Europe and Asia and found that favorable views of America have plummeted in the last two decades — most dramatically since 2016. And confidence in Donald Trump "to do the right thing in foreign affairs" is even worse.

For example, while 59% of South Korea look favorably at the U.S., one of the highest approval ratings of any country, only 17% trust Mr. Trump with world affairs. In Germany, 26% have a positive view of the U.S. (down from 78% in 2000) but only 10% for Mr. Trump. Similar views were registered in Britain, France and Australia.

Of world leaders, Mr. Trump, Russia's Vladimir Putin and China's Xi Jinping were rated the least respected. Mr. Trump had the lowest score, with a disapproval rating of 83%, behind Mr. Putin's 73% and Mr. Xi's 78%.
The Trump administration's hapless response to the coronavirus contributed to the low opinion. With the U.S. having 20% of deaths (217,000) yet less than 5% of the global population, only 15% of respondents felt the United States "had done a good job."

But the decline stems from far more than the administration's COVID-19 failure.

Mr. Trump's serial lying, his trampling on the rule of law, threats to cling to power if defeated in November and constant attempts to divide the country by embracing white supremacy are widely condemned around the world — not just in the U.S. The past American status as a beacon for values-based democracy has been shattered by Mr. Trump's conduct.

Mr. Trump's foreign policy has been distinguished by misshapen goals and few results — from his futile love affair with North Korea's dictator Kim Jung Un to applauding and then bashing China's Mr. Xi to his submissive kowtowing to Russia's Mr. Putin. He has alienated America's closest friends and members of the NATO alliance. He still calls climate change "a Chinese hoax" — despite the opposite conclusions of most all scientists.

He has withdrawn the United States from one critical treaty after another, prompting Republican strategist Richard Haass to call Mr. Trump's foreign policy the "Withdrawal Doctrine."

The damage to America's reputation, notably our "soft power" — the appeal of our values, free speech, respect for human rights and a vibrant culture — may take decades to reverse.

Mr. Trump's achievements are scant. The two small Arab countries that recognized Israel already had extensive ties to the Jewish state. "Build the wall?" Mexico paid not a cent, and the administration lifted funds from the Pentagon for its partial completion.

Mr. Trump has had a revolving door of national security leaders, starting with respected individuals such as Gen. James Mattis and former GOP Sen. Dan Coats, now staffed by third-rate officials. Rather than strengthen the military, he has repeatedly insulted senior general and admirals as "dopes and babies." He has downgraded the role of diplomacy, sought to destroy the State Department and maligned CIA officers as "Nazis."

Four years ago, 50 national security leaders — all Republicans — forecast that Mr. Trump would be the "most reckless" and "most dangerous" president in American history. Today, 70 of these leaders, along with 489 military leaders, condemn his leadership.

Is it any wonder the United States is no longer respected in the world?

The Oct. 4 Book World excerpt from Carlos Lozada's book, "What Were We Thinking: A Brief Intellectual History of the Trump Era," said not a word about President Trump's erratic, reckless and damaging foreign policy and failure to secure our national security interests. From a bizarre and possibly treasonous embrace of Russia, described in his own administration's National Security Strategy as a perilous foe, to his complete failure in dealing with nuclear weapons issues with North Korea and Iran, to his denial of climate change, to withdrawal from one multilateral treaty after another, Trump has proved to be just what 50 former national security officials who served under Republican presidents predicted in August 2016: "the most reckless" president in U.S. history. More than 70 such men and women say that today, plus nearly 500 top military leaders.

Virtually every respected national security leader in the country — former secretaries of defense and state and heads of national intelligence — has condemned Trump's performance over nearly four years. Many have quit the administration in disgust at his lack of competence. The recent Pew Research Center survey of global views of the United States verifies the collapse in respect for this country under Trump.

Because the article was "adapted" from Lozada's book, it is impossible to know whether that volume contains any mention of these critical issues.

Frederic B. Hill, *Arrowsic, Maine*
The writer was foreign affairs director for
Sen. Charles McC. Mathias Jr. (R-Md.). He is the author
of "Dereliction of Duty: The Failed Presidency

Notes

1. Rucker, Philip and Leonigg, Carol. *A Very Stable Genius*. New York – Penguin Press, 2020. P. 138.

2. Rolen Bergman, one of Israel's most respected journalists, broke the story about Trump's reckless disclosure to Russian foreign minister, Sergei Lavrov, in May 2017. Bergman wrote that Israel's government and intelligence leaders considered the disclosure "a blunt violation" of long-standing agreements and trust between the U.S. and Israel, and said they would review all intelligence cooperation with Washington. (The New York Times, PBS and Yedioth Ahronoh, Israel's largest newspaper, May, 2017).

3. George Shultz made this comment about President Trump and the Trump administration's failures on nuclear arms issues during a meeting of the Commonwealth Club of California, May 20, 2020. Without naming Trump, Shultz said the primary fault for the lapse in commitment to this critical matter did not lie with the Russian leader, Vladimir Putin, but in Washington. "Get going, U.S." he said at one point during the program.

4. *Muldoon*. A colorful term applied to political hangers-on, mainly dim camp-followers of any party stripe, and virtually unknown outside Baltimore and the state of Maryland. Its popular use stemmed from the famous early 20th century columns of Frank R. Kent of The Baltimore Sun who used "muldoons" for politicians who could be counted on "for their vote on the party side of every issue, regardless of facts, figures and argument." The paper's noted cartoonist, Richard "Moco" Yardley, also peopled his brilliant political cartoons with little round men, wearing derby hats, all marked "1/6 boss," "1/4 boss," "1/8" boss" to delineate how many factions each one ruled in the city or state.

Acknowledgments

I am deeply indebted to a number of outstanding editors and op-ed page editors for several leading American newspapers who have published my articles over the last 15 years.

I would like to express my appreciation for the support and superb editing skills of Susan Young (and several op-ed page editors) at the *Bangor Daily News*; Elizabeth Souder at *The Dallas Morning News*, Tricia Bishop at *The Baltimore Sun* and her successor, Andrea McDaniels, Greg Kesich at the Portland Press Herald and John Swinconeck, of the *Bath Brunswick Times-Record*. All superb newspapers, and exemplary, daily proof of the value of the print press despite the harrowing inroads of social media and a narcissistic president who called any of them that criticized him "an enemy of the people." As a reminder, that was a phrase made famous by none other than Josef Stalin, the brutal dictator of the former Soviet Union.

I want to thank several colleagues and friends who collaborated with me on several articles, lending their expertise on subjects that I knew far less about.

First and foremost, I am grateful for the enduring friendship and expertise of James E. Goodby, chief architect of the Limited Nuclear Test Ban Treaty, vice-chair of the U.S. Delegation to the Strategic Arms Reduction Talks (START) with the Soviet Union, and ambassador to Finland. Jim and I worked together on many gaming exercises and senior-level roundtable discussions at the State Department, and he and I collaborated later on nearly a dozen articles on nuclear weapons and other issues.

I also have enjoyed writing articles with Col. Sam Gardiner, a colleague at the National Defense University and remarkably

gifted leader of far-seeing wargaming exercises for the U.S.
government and private organizations, and with a close personal
friend, Walter Kozumbo, a very astute scientist.

This volume could not have been completed without outstanding
research, editing and technical support from Lauren Leatham,
Bowdoin/Cornell class of 2023 and the technical skills and
patience of Leilani Goggin, a genius with computers.

I am indebted to two outstanding scholars and fellow graduates of
Bowdoin. Cal Mackenzie, a Colby College professor, Vietnam
veteran and author of 20 books on American history and politics,
and now an outstanding photographer, tutored me through the
process of self-publishing. Also to Chris Potholm, my close friend
and classmate, Bowdoin professor of government for five decades,
and author of 20 or more books on everything from the strategy
and vicissitudes of war to African governance to Maine politics.

I also am thankful for the many friends and colleagues in the
world of journalism and diplomacy whose writing, editing and
lasting friendship helped me to better understand complex
international issues and write passable prose about them. They
start with my mother's cousin, Richard Matthews Hallet, a
Harvard-trained lawyer who cast his law career to the winds and
lived an adventurous life on the high seas and remote lands,
writing nearly 200 short stories for the leading magazines of the
early 20th century, many novels and a rollicking autobiography. It
was "Uncle" Richard who first suggested I might be happier in the
newspaper world than pursuing a legal career. They include, in
the newspaper world, Paul Banker, the managing editor of *The
Sun* who first offered me a chance, Scott Sullivan, Jeff Price, Bill
Schmick, Tom Edsall, Gilbert Lewthwaite, Steve Broening, Carl
Leubsdorf, Steve Luxenberg, Ray Jenkins, Dick Basoco, Joe Sterne,

Frank DeFilippo, David Brown, David Treadwell, and many others.

In the diplomatic, national security and legal fields, I want to recognize enduring support and wise counsel from Sen. Chris Van Hollen (D., MD.), Ambassador Laurence E. Pope, Ambassador Frederic Hof, Col. Lawrence Wilkerson, Ambassador Thomas R. Pickering, Hans Binnendijk, Ambassador Stephen Low, Ambassador Lawrence Taylor, Ambassador Dennis Kux, Ambassador Ruth Davis, Ambassador Teresita Schaffer, Ambassador William Burns, Robert Hopper, Randy Cheek, Col. Dennis Murphy, Col. Craig Bollenberg, Col. Mike Harwood, Julian Lapides and Stephen Sachs.

Last but first, I could not have endeavored to tackle these issues and other projects without the enduring patience, technical skills and love of my wife, Marty, whom I am so lucky to have met not long after I landed at *The Baltimore Sun*.

About the Author

Frederic B. Hill was a reporter, correspondent and editorial writer for *The Baltimore Sun,* including tours as Bureau Chief in London and Paris, covering Europe and southern Africa. He then served as Foreign Affairs Director for Sen. Charles McC. Mathias, Jr. (R., MD) in 1985 and 1986.

He helped establish and then headed an office in the Department of State that conducted policy planning exercises (wargames) and senior-level discussions on national security and global issues from 1986 to 2006.

A native of Maine and graduate of Bowdoin College, he is the author of *Ships, Swindlers and Scalded Hogs, the Rise and Fall of the Crooker Shipyard in Bath, Maine* (Down East Books, 2016) and co-editor of *The Life of Kings; The Baltimore Sun and the Golden Age of the American Newspaper* (Rowman & Littlefield, 2016). *A Flick of Sunshine,* with Alexander J. Hill, is scheduled to be published in fall, 2020 (Lyons Press), as is *On The Wallaby, The Short Stories of Richard Matthews Hallet.*

Senator Charles McC. Mathias, Jr. and the author, May, 1985.

* 9 7 9 8 6 6 5 7 2 6 3 8 0 *